THE

Charity Sermon;

OR,

CHARACTER

AND

RULE OF HOLY LIFE.

BY REV. GEORGE ELLIOTT.

BOSTON
JAMES B. DOW, PUBLISHER.
1840

THE
Country Parson:

HIS

CHARACTER

AND

RULE OF HOLY LIFE.

BY REV. GEORGE HERBERT.

BOSTON:
JAMES B. DOW, PUBLISHER.
1842.

This scarce antiquarian book is included in our special *Legacy Reprint Series*. In the interest of creating a more extensive selection of rare historical book reprints, we have chosen to reproduce this title even though it may possibly have occasional imperfections such as missing and blurred pages, missing text, poor pictures, markings, dark backgrounds and other reproduction issues beyond our control. Because this work is culturally important, we have made it available as a part of our commitment to protecting, preserving and promoting the world's literature. Thank you for your understanding.

CONTENTS

OF THE

Country Parson.

CHAP.
I. Of a Pastor,	287
II. Their Diversities,	288
III. The Parson's Life,	289
IV. The Parson's Knowledge,	291
V. The Parson's Accessary Knowledges,	293
VI. The Parson Praying,	294
VII. The Parson Preaching,	296
VIII. The Parson on Sundays,	300
IX. The Parson's State of Life,	302
X. The Parson in his House,	305
XI. The Parson's Courtesy,	310
XII. The Parson's Charity,	311
XIII. The Parson's Church,	313
XIV. The Parson in Circuit,	315
XV. The Parson Comforting,	318
XVI. The Parson a Father,	319
XVII. The Parson in Journey,	319
XVIII. The Parson in Sentinel,	321
XIX. The Parson in Reference,	322
XX. The Parson in God's Stead,	324

CONTENTS.

CHAP.
XXI. The Parson Catechising, . . . 325
XXII. The Parson in Sacraments, . . . 328
XXIII. The Parson's Completeness, . . 331
XXIV. The Parson Arguing, ... 334
XXV. The Parson Punishing, . . . 335
XXVI. The Parson's Eye, ... 336
XXVII. The Parson in Mirth, . . . 340
XXVIII. The Parson in Contempt, . . . 341
XXIX. The Parson with his Church Wardens, 343
XXX. The Parson's Consideration of Providence, 344
XXXI. The Parson in Liberty, . . . 346
XXXII. The Parson's Surveys, ... 348
XXXIII. The Parson's Library, . . . 353
XXXIV. The Parson's Dexterity in applying of Remedies, ... 355
XXXV. The Parson's Condescending, . . 360
XXXVI. The Parson Blessing, . . . 361
XXXVII. Concerning Detraction, . . . 364
The Author's Prayer before Sermon, . . 366
A Prayer after Sermon, ... 368

THE AUTHOR TO THE READER.

BEING desirous, through the mercy of God, to please him, for whom I am and live, and who giveth me my desires and performances; and considering with myself, that the way to please him is to feed my flock diligently and faithfully, since our Saviour hath made that the argument of a pastor's love; I have resolved to set down the form and character of a true pastor, that I may have a mark to aim at: which also I will set as high as I can, since he shoots higher that threatens the moon, than he that aims at a tree. Not that I think, if a man do not all which is here expressed, he presently sins, and displeases God; but that it is a good strife to go as far as we can in pleasing of him, who hath done so much for us. The Lord prosper the intention to myself, and others, who may not despise my poor labors, but add to those points which I have observed, until the book grow to a complete pastoral.

GEORGE HERBERT.

1632.

A Priest to the Temple:

OR,

THE COUNTRY PARSON.

CHAPTER I.

Of a Pastor.

A PASTOR is the deputy of Christ, for the reducing of man to the obedience of God. This definition is evident, and contains the direct steps of pastoral duty and authority. For, first, man fell from God by disobedience. Secondly, Christ is the glorious instrument of God for the revoking of man. Thirdly, Christ being not to continue on earth, but, after he had fulfilled the work of reconciliation, to be received up into heaven, he constituted deputies in his place; and these are priests. And therefore St. Paul, in the beginning of his epistles, professeth this: and, in the first to the Colossians, plainly avoucheth that he *fills up that which is behind of the afflictions of Christ in his flesh, for his body's sake, which is the church.* Wherein is contained the complete definition of a minister.

Out of this charter of the priesthood may be plainly gathered both the dignity thereof, and the duty. The dignity, in that a priest *may do* that which Christ did, and by his authority, and as his vicegerent. The duty, in that a priest *is to do* that which Christ did, and after his manner, both for doctrine and life.

CHAPTER II.

Their Diversities.

Of Pastors (intending mine own nation only; and also therein setting aside the reverend prelates of the church, to whom this discourse ariseth not), some live in the universities; some in noble houses; some in parishes, residing on their cures.

Of those that live in the universities, some live there in office; whose rule is that of the apostle (Rom. xii. 6); *Having gifts, differing according to the grace that is given to us, whether prophecy, let us prophesy according to the proportion of faith; or ministry, let us wait on our ministering; or he that teacheth, on teaching, &c.; he that ruleth, let him do it with diligence, &c.* Some in a preparatory way; whose aim and labor must be, not only to get knowledge, but to subdue and mortify all lusts and affections; and not to think that, when they have read the fathers or schoolmen, a minister is made and the thing done. The greatest and hardest preparation is within. For *unto the ungodly, saith God, why dost thou preach my laws, and takest my covenant in thy mouth?* (Ps. l. 16.)

Those that live in noble houses are called chaplains; whose duty and obligation being the same to the houses they live in, as a parson's to his parish, in describing the one (which is indeed the bent of my discourse), the other will be manifest. Let not chaplains think themselves so free, as many of them do; and, because they have different names, think their office different. Doubtless they are parsons of the families they live in, and are entertained to that end, either by an open or implicit covenant. Before they are in orders, they may be received for companions, or discoursers; but after a man is once minister, he cannot agree to come into any house where he shall not exercise what he is, unless he forsake his plough and look back. Wherefore they are not to be over-submissive and base, but to keep up with the lord and lady of the house, and to preserve a boldness with them and all, even so far as reproof to their very face, when occasion calls; but seasonably, and discreetly. They who do not thus, while they remember their earthly lord, do much forget their heavenly; they wrong the priesthood, neglect their duty, and shall be so far from that which they seek with their over-submissiveness and cringings, that they shall ever be despised. They who, for the hope of promotion, neglect any necessary admonition or reproof, sell (with Judas) their Lord and Master.

CHAPTER III.

The Parson's Life.

THE Country Parson is exceeding exact in his life; being holy, just, prudent, temperate, bold, grave, in all his ways. And because the two highest points of life, wherein a Christian is most seen, are patience, and mortification; patience in regard of afflictions, mortification in regard of lusts and affections, and the stupifying and deadening of all the clamorous powers of the soul; therefore he hath throughly studied these, that he may be an absolute master and commander of himself, for all the purposes which God hath ordained him.

Yet in these points, he labors most in those things which are most apt to scandalize his parish. And first, because country people live hardly, and therefore (as feeling their own sweat, and consequently knowing the price of money) are offended much with any who by hard usage increase their travail, the country parson is very circumspect in avoiding all covetousness; neither being greedy to get, nor niggardly to keep, nor troubled to lose, any worldly wealth; but, in all his words and actions, slighting and disesteeming it; even to a wondering that the world should so much value wealth, which in the day of wrath hath not one drachm of comfort for us.—Secondly, because luxury is a very visible sin, the parson is very careful to avoid all the kinds thereof: but especially that of drinking, because it is the most popular vice; into which if he come, he prostitutes himself both to shame and sin, and, by having *fellowship with the unfruitful works of darkness*, he disableth himself of authority to *reprove them*. For sins make all equal whom they find together; and then *they* are worst, who ought to be best. Neither is it for the servant of Christ to haunt inns, or taverns, or alehouses, to the dishonor of his person and office. The parson doth not so, but orders his life in such a fashion, that, when death takes him, as the Jews and Judas did Christ, he may say as *he* did, *I sat daily with you teaching in the temple*.—Thirdly, because country people (as indeed all honest men) do much esteem their word, it being the life of buying and selling and dealing in the world, therefore the parson is very strict in keeping his word, though it be to his own hindrance; as knowing that, if he be not so, he will quickly be discovered and disrespected: neither will they believe him in the pulpit, whom they cannot trust in his conversation.—As for oaths, and apparel, the disorders thereof are also very manifest. The parson's yea is yea, and nay, nay: and his apparel plain, but reverend, and clean, without spots, or dust, or smell; the purity of his mind breaking out, and dilating itself even to his body, clothes, and habitation.

CHAPTER IV.

The Parson's Knowledge.

THE Country Parson is full of all knowledge. They say, it is an ill mason that refuseth any stone: and there is no knowledge, but, in a skilful hand, serves either positively as it is, or else to illustrate some other knowledge. He condescends even to the knowledge of tillage and pasturage, and makes great use of them in teaching; because people by what they understand, are best led to what they understand not.

But the chief and top of his knowledge consists in the book of books, the storehouse and magazine of life and comfort, THE HOLY SCRIPTURES. There he sucks, and lives. In the scriptures he finds four things; precepts for life, doctrines for knowledge, examples for illustration, and promises for comfort. These he hath digested severally.

But for the understanding of these, the means he useth are—First, A HOLY LIFE; remembering what his Master saith, that *if any do God's will, he shall know of the doctrine* (John vii.); and assuring himself, that wicked men, however learned, do not know the scriptures, because they feel them not, and because they are not understood but with the same Spirit that writ them.—The second means is PRAYER; which, if it be necessary even in temporal things, how much more in things of another world, where *the well is deep, and we have nothing* of ourselves *to draw with?* Wherefore he ever begins the reading of the scripture with some short ejaculation; as, *Lord, open mine eyes, that I may see the wondrous things of thy law.*—The third means is A DILIGENT COLLATION of scripture with scripture. For, all truth being consonant to itself, and all being penned by one and the self-same Spirit, it cannot be, but that an industrious and judicious comparing of place with place must be a singular help for the right understanding of the scriptures. To this may be added, the consideration of any text with the coherence thereof, touching what goes before, and what follows after; as also the scope of the Holy Ghost. When the apostles would have called down fire from heaven, they were reproved, as ignorant of what spirit they were. For the law required one thing, and the gospel another; yet as diverse, not as repugnant: therefore the spirit of both is to be considered and weighed.—The fourth means are COMMENTERS AND FATHERS, who have handled the places controverted; which the parson by no means refuseth. As he doth not so study others as to neglect the grace of God in himself, and what the Holy Spirit teacheth him; so doth he assure himself, that God in all ages hath had his servants, to whom he hath revealed his truth, as well as to him: and that as one country doth not bear all things, that there may be a commerce; so neither hath God opened, or will open, all to one, that there may be a traffic in knowledge between the servants of God, for the planting both of love and humility. Wherefore he hath one comment, at least, upon every book of scripture; and, ploughing with this, and his own meditations, he enters into the secrets of God treasured in the holy scripture.

CHAPTER V.

The Parson's Accessary Knowledges.

THE Country Parson hath read the fathers also, and the schoolmen, and the later writers, or a good proportion of all: out of all which he hath compiled a book, and body of divinity, which is the storehouse of his sermons, and which he preacheth all his life, but diversely clothed, illustrated, and enlarged. For though the world is full of such composures, yet every man's own is fittest, readiest, and most savory to him. Besides, this being to be done in his younger and preparatory times, it is an honest joy ever after to look upon his well-spent hours.

This body he made, by way of expounding the church catechism; to which all divinity may easily be reduced. For, it being indifferent in itself to choose any method, that is best to be chosen of which there is likeliest to be most use. Now catechising being a work of singular and admirable benefit to the church of God, and a thing required under canonical obedience, the expounding of our catechism must needs be the most useful form. Yet hath the parson, besides this laborious work, a slighter form of catechising, fitter for country people;

according as his audience is, so he useth one, or other; or sometimes both, if his audience be intermixed.

He greatly esteems also of cases of conscience; wherein he is much versed. And indeed, herein is the greatest ability of a parson; to lead his people exactly in the ways of truth, so that they neither decline to the right hand nor to the left. Neither let any think this a slight thing. For every one hath not digested, when it is a sin to take something for money lent, or when not; when it is fault to discover another's fault, or when not; when the affections of the soul in desiring and procuring increase of means, or honor, be a sin of covetousness or ambition, and when not; when the appetites of the body in eating, drinking, sleep, and the pleasure that comes with sleep, be sins of gluttony, drunkenness, sloth, lust, and when not; and so in many circumstances of actions. Now if a shepherd know not which grass will bane, or which not, how is he fit to be a shepherd? Wherefore the parson hath throughly canvassed all the particulars of human actions; at least all those which he observeth are most incident to his parish.

CHAPTER VI.

The Parson Praying.

THE Country Parson, when he is to read divine services, composeth himself to all possible reverence; lifting up his heart, and hands, and eyes, and using all other gestures which may express a hearty and unfeigned devotion. This he doth—First, as being truly touched and amazed with the majesty of God, before whom he then presents himself; yet not as himself alone, but as presenting with himself the whole congregation; whose sins he then bears, and brings with his own to the heavenly altar, to be bathed and washed in the sacred laver of Christ's blood. Secondly, as this is the true reason of his inward fear, so he is content to express this outwardly to the utmost of his power; that, being first affected himself, he may affect also his people; knowing that no sermon moves them so much to reverence (which they forget again when they come to pray), as a devout behaviour in the very act of praying. Accordingly his voice is humble, his words treatable and slow; yet not so slow neither, as to let the fervency of the supplicant hang and die between speaking; but, with a grave liveliness, between fear and zeal, pausing yet pressing, he performs his duty.

Besides his example, he, having often instructed his people how to carry themselves in divine service, exacts of them all possible reverence: by no means enduring either talking, or sleeping, or gazing, or leaning, or half-kneeling, or any undutiful behaviour in them; but causing them, when they sit, or stand, or kneel, to do all in a straight and steady posture, as attending to what is done in the church, and every one, man and child, answering aloud, both·Amen, and all other answers which are on the clerk's and people's part to answer. Which answers also are to be done, not in a huddling or slubbering fashion—gaping or scratching the head, or spitting, even in the midst of their answer—but gently and plausibly, thinking what they say; so that while they answer "As it was in the beginning," &c. they meditate as they speak, that God hath ever had his people that have glorified him, as well as now, and that he shall have so for ever. And the like in other answers. This is that which the apostle calls a *reasonable service* (Rom. xii.), when we speak not as parrots without reason, or offer up such sacrifices as they did of old, which was of beasts devoid of reason; but when we use our reason, and apply our powers to the service of him that gives them.

If there be any of the gentry or nobility of the parish, who sometimes make it a piece of state not to come at the beginning of service with their poor neighbors, but at mid-prayers, both to their own loss, and of theirs also who gaze upon them when they come in, and neglect the present service of God; he by no means suffers it, but after divers gentle admonitions, if they persevere, he causes them to be presented. Or if the poor churchwardens be affrighted with their greatness (notwithstanding his instruction that they ought not to be so, but even to let the world sink, so they do their duty), he presents them himself; only protesting to them, that not any ill-will draws him to it, but the debt and obligation of his calling, being to obey God rather than men.

CHAPTER VII.

The Parson Preaching.

THE Country Parson preacheth constantly. The pulpit is his joy and his throne. If he at any time intermit, it is either for want of health; or against some festival, that he may the better celebrate it; or for the variety of the hearers, that he may be heard at his return more attentively. When he intermits, he is ever very well supplied by some able man; who treads in his steps, and will not throw down what he hath built; whom also he entreats to press some point that he himself hath often urged with no great success, that so *in the mouth of two or three witnesses the truth may be* more *established.*

When he preacheth, he procures attention by all possible art: both by earnestness of speech; it being natural to men to think, that where is much earnestness, there is somewhat worth hearing: and by a diligent and busy cast of his eye on his auditors, with letting them know that he marks who observes, and who not: and with particularizing of his speech now to the younger sort, then to the elder, now to the poor, and now to the rich— " This is for you, and this is for you;"—for particulars ever touch, and awake, more than generals. Herein also he serves himself of the judgments of God: as of those of ancient times, so especially of the late ones; and those most, which are nearest to his parish; for people are very attentive at such discourses, and think it behoves them to be so, when God is so near them, and even over their heads. Sometimes he tells them stories and sayings of others, according as his text invites him: for them also men heed, and remember better than exhortations; which, though earnest, yet often die with the sermon, especially with country people; which are thick, and heavy, and hard to raise to a point of zeal and fervency, and need a mountain of fire to kindle them; but stories and sayings they will well remember. He often tells them, that sermons are dangerous things; that none goes out of church as he came in, but either better or worse; that none is careless before his Judge; and that the word of God shall judge us.

By these and other means the parson procures attention; but the character of his sermon is HOLINESS.

He is not witty, or learned, or eloquent, but HOLY:—a character that Hermogenes never dreamed of, and therefore he could give no precepts thereof. But it is gained,—First, by choosing texts of devotion, not controversy; moving and ravishing texts, whereof the scriptures are full.—Secondly, by dipping and seasoning all our words and sentences in our hearts before they come into our mouths; truly affecting, and cordially expressing all that we say: so that the auditors may plainly perceive that every word is heart-deep.—Thirdly, by turning often, and making many apostrophes to God; as, "O Lord! bless my people, and teach them this point!" or, "O my Master, on whose errand I come, let me hold my peace, and do thou speak thyself; for thou art love; and when thou teachest, all are scholars." Some such irradiations scatteringly in the sermon, carry great holiness in them. The prophets are admirable in this. So Isa. lxiv.; *Oh, thou that wouldest rend the heavens, that thou wouldest come down,* &c. And Jeremy (chap. x.), after he had complained of the desolation of Israel, turns to God suddenly, *O Lord! I know that the way of man is not in himself,* &c.—Fourthly, by frequent wishes of the people's good, and joying therein; though he himself were, with St. Paul, *even sacrificed upon the service of their faith.* For there is no greater sign of holiness, than the procuring and rejoicing in another's good. And herein St. Paul excelled, in all his epistles. How did he put the Romans *in all his prayers* (Rom. i. 9); and *ceased not to give thanks* for the Ephesians (Eph. i. 16); and for the Corinthians (1 Cor. i. 4); and for the Philippians *made request with joy* (Phil. i. 4); and is in contention for them whether to live or die, be with them or Christ (ver. 23); which, setting aside his care of his flock, were a madness to

THE COUNTRY PARSON. 19

doubt of. What an admirable epistle is the second to the Corinthians! How full of affections! He joys, and he is sorry; he grieves, and he glories! Never was there such a care of a flock expressed, save in the great Shepherd of the fold, who first shed tears over Jerusalem, and afterwards blood. Therefore this care may be learned there, and then woven into sermons; which will make them appear exceeding reverend and holy.—Lastly, by an often urging of the presence and majesty of God; by these, or such like speeches—" Oh, let us take heed what we do! God sees us; he sees whether I speak as I ought, or you hear as you ought; he sees hearts, as we see faces. He is among us; for if we be here, he must be here; since we are here by him, and without him could not be here." Then, turning the discourse to his majesty,—" and he is a great God, and terrible; as great in mercy, so great in judgment! There are but two devouring elements, fire and water; he hath both in him. *His voice is as the sound of many waters,* (Rev. i.); and he himself *is a consuming fire.*" (Heb. xii.)—Such discourses shew very holy.

The parson's method in handling of a text consists of two parts:—First, a plain and evident declaration of the meaning of the text;—and Secondly, some choice observations, drawn out of the whole text, as it lies entire and unbroken in the scripture itself. This he thinks natural, and sweet, and grave. Whereas the other way, of crumbling a text into small parts, (as, the person speaking or spoken to, the subject, and object, and the like,) hath neither in it sweetness, nor gravity, nor variety; since the words apart are not scripture, but a dictionary, and may be considered alike in all the scripture.

The parson exceeds not an hour in preaching, because

20   THE COUNTRY PARSON.

all ages have thought that a competency: and he that profits not in that time, will less afterwards; the same affection which made him not profit before, making him then weary; and so he grows from not relishing, to loathing.

CHAPTER VIII.
The Parson on Sundays.

THE Country Parson, as soon as he awakes on Sunday morning, presently falls to work, and seems to himself so as a market-man is, when the market-day comes; or a shop-keeper, when customers use to come in. His thoughts are full of making the best of the day, and contriving it to his best gains. To this end, besides his ordinary prayers, he makes a peculiar one for a blessing on the exercises of the day; "that nothing befall him unworthy of that Majesty before which he is to present himself, but that all may be done with reverence to his glory, and with edification to his flock; humbly beseeching his Master, that how or whenever he punish him, it be not in his ministry." Then he turns to request for his people, "that the Lord would be pleased to sanctify them all; that they may come with holy hearts, and awful minds, into the congregation; and that the good God would pardon all those who come with less prepared hearts than they ought."

This done, he sets himself to the consideration of the duties of the day; and if there be any extraordinary addition to the customary exercises, either from the time of the year, or from the state, or from God by a child born, or dead, or any other accident, he contrives how and in what manner to induce it to the best advantage. Afterwards, when the hour calls, with his family attending him, he goes to the church; at his first entrance humbly adoring and worshipping the invisible majesty and presence of Almighty God, and blessing the people, either openly, or to himself. Then, having read divine service twice fully, and preached in the morning, and catechised in the afternoon, he thinks he hath in some measure, according to poor and frail man, discharged the public duties of the congregation. The rest of the day he spends either in reconciling neighbors that are at variance; or in visiting the sick; or in exhortations to some of his flock by themselves, whom his sermons cannot, or do not, reach. And every one is more awaked, when we come and say, *Thou art the man.* This way he finds exceeding useful, and winning: and these exhortations he calls his privy purse; even as princes have theirs, besides their public disbursements. At night he thinks it a fit time, both suitable to the joy of the day, and without hindrance to public duties, either to entertain some of his neighbors, or to be entertained of them: where he takes occasion to discourse of such things as are both profitable and pleasant, and to raise up their minds to apprehend God's good blessing to our church and state; that order is kept in the one, and peace in the other, without disturbance or interruption of public divine offices.

As he opened the day with prayer, so he closeth it; humbly beseeching the Almighty "to pardon and accept our poor services, and to improve them, that we may grow therein: and that our feet may be like hind's feet, ever climbing up higher and higher unto him."

CHAPTER IX.

The Parson's State of Life.

The Country Parson, considering that virginity is a higher state than matrimony, and that the ministry requires the best and highest things, is rather unmarried than married. But yet, as the temper of his body may be, or as the temper of his parish may be, where he may have occasion to converse with women, and that among suspicious men, and other like circumstances considered, he is rather married than unmarried. Let him communicate the thing often by prayer unto God; and as his grace shall direct him, so let him proceed.

If he be unmarried, and keep house, he hath not a woman in his house; but finds opportunities of having his meat dressed and other services done by men servants at home, and his linen washed abroad. If he be unmarried, and sojourn, he never talks with any woman alone, but in the audience of others; and that seldom; and then also in a serious manner, never jestingly or sportfully. He is very circumspect in all companies, both of his behavior, speech, and very looks; knowing himself to be both suspected and envied. If he *stand steadfast in his heart, having no necessity, but hath power over his own will, and hath so decreed in his heart, that he will keep himself a virgin,* he spends his days in fasting and prayer, and blesseth God for the gift of continency; knowing that it can no way be preserved, but only by those means by which at first it was obtained. He therefore thinks it not enough for him to observe the fasting days of the church, and the daily prayers enjoined him by authority, which he observeth out of humble conformity and obedience; but adds to them, out of choice and devotion, some other days for fasting, and hours for prayers. And by these he keeps his body tame, serviceable, and healthful; and his soul fervent, active, young, and lusty as an eagle. He often readeth the lives of the primitive monks, hermits, and virgins; and wondereth not so much at their patient suffering, and cheerful dying under persecuting emperors (though that indeed be very admirable), as at their daily temperance, abstinence, watchings, and constant prayers, and mortifications, in times of peace and prosperity. To put on the profound humility and the exact temperance of our Lord Jesus, with other exemplary virtues of that sort, and to keep them on in the sunshine and noon of prosperity, he findeth to be as necessary and as difficult, at least, as to be clothed with perfect patience and Christian fortitude in the cold midnight storms of persecution and adversity. He keepeth his watch and ward, night and day, against the proper and peculiar temptations of his state of life; which are principally these two, spiritual pride, and impurity of heart. Against these ghostly enemies he girdeth up his loins, keeps the imagination from roving, puts on the whole armor of God; and, by the virtue of the shield of faith, he is *not afraid of the pestilence that walketh in darkness,* (carnal impurity,) *nor of the sickness that destroyeth at noon-day,* (ghostly pride and self-conceit.) Other temptations he hath, which, like mortal enemies, may sometimes disquiet him likewise; for the human soul, being bounded and kept in her sensitive faculty, will run out more or less in her intellectual. Original concupiscence is such an active thing, by reason of continual inward or outward temptations, that it is ever attempting or doing one mischief or other. Ambition, or untimely desire of promotion to an higher state or place, under color of accommodation, or necessary provision, is a common temptation to men of any eminency, especially being single men. Curiosity in prying into high, speculative, and unprofitable questions, is another great stumbling-block to the holiness of scholars. These, and many other *spiritual wickednesses in high places* doth the parson fear, or experiment, or both: and that much more being single, than if he were married; for then commonly the stream of temptations is turned another way, into covetousness, love of pleasure or ease, or the like.—If the parson be unmarried, and means to continue so, he doth at least as much as hath been said.

If he be married, the choice of his wife was made rather by his ear, than by his eye; his judgment, not his affection, found out a fit wife for him, whose humble and liberal disposition he preferred before beauty, riches, or honor. He knew that (the good instrument of God to bring women to heaven) a wise and loving husband could, out of humility, produce any special grace of faith, patience, meekness, love, obedience, &c.; and, out of liberality, make her fruitful in all good works. As he is just in all things, so is he to his wife also; counting nothing so much his own, as that he may be unjust unto it. Therefore he gives her respect, both afore her servants and others, and half at least of the government of the house; reserving so much of the affairs, as serve for a diversion for him; yet never so giving over the reins, but that he sometimes looks how things go, demanding an account,—but not by the way of an account. And this must be done the oftener or the seldomer, according as he is satisfied of his wife's discretion.

CHAPTER I.

The Parson in his House.

The Parson is very exact in the governing of his house, making it a copy and model for his parish. He knows the temper and pulse of every person in his house; and, accordingly, either meets with their vices, or advanceth their virtues.—His wife is either religious, or night and day he is winning her to it. Instead of the qualities of the world, he requires only three of her. First, a training up of her children and maids in the fear of God; with prayers, and catechising, and all religious duties. Secondly, a curing and healing of all wounds and sores with her own hands; which skill either she brought with her, or he takes care she shall learn it of some religious neighbor. Thirdly, a providing for her family in such sort, as that neither they want a competent sustentation, nor her husband be brought in debt.

His children he first makes Christians, and then commonwealth's men: the one he owes to his heavenly country, the other to his earthly, having no title to either, except he do good to both. Therefore, having seasoned them with all piety—not only of words, in praying, and reading; but in actions, in visiting other sick children, and tending their wounds; and sending his charity by them to the poor, and sometimes giving them a little money to do it of themselves, that they get a delight in it, and enter favor with God, who weighs even children's actions (1 Kings, xiv. 12, 13),—he afterwards turns his care to fit all their dispositions with some calling; not sparing the eldest, but giving him the prerogative of his father's profession, which happily for his other children he is not able to do. Yet in binding them apprentices (in case he think fit to do so), he takes care not to put them into vain trades, unbefitting the reverence of their father's calling: such as are taverns for men, and lace-making for women; because those trades, for the most part, serve but the vices and vanities of the world, which he is to deny, and not augment. However, he resolves with himself never to omit any present good deed of charity, in consideration of providing a stock for his children: but assures himself that money, thus lent to God, is placed surer for his children's advantage, than if it were given to the chamber of London. Good deeds and good breeding are his two great stocks for his children; if God give any thing above those, and not spent in them, he blesseth God, and lays it out as he sees cause.

His servants are all religious: and were it not his duty to have them so, it were his profit; for none are so well served, as by religious servants; both because they do best, and because what they do is blessed, and prospers. After religion, he teaches them, that three things make a complete servant:—truth, and diligence, and neatness or cleanliness.—Those that can read, are allowed times for it; and those that cannot, are taught: for all in his house are either teachers, or learners, or both; so that his family is a school of religion: and they all account, that to teach the ignorant is the greatest alms. Even the walls are not idle; but something is written or painted there, which may excite the reader to a thought of piety: especially the 101st Psalm; which is expressed in a fair table, as being the rule of a family. And when they go abroad, his wife among her neighbors is the beginning of good discourses; his children, among children; his servants, among other servants. So that as in the house of those that are skilled in music, all are musicians; so in the house of a preacher, all are preachers.—He suffers not a lie or equivocation by any means in his house, but counts it the art and secret of governing, to preserve a directness and open plainness in all things: so that all his house knows that there is no help for a fault done, but confession.—He himself, or his wife, takes account of sermons, and how every one profits, comparing this year with the last. And, besides the common prayers of the family, he straitly requires of all to pray by themselves, before they sleep at night, and stir out in the morning; and knows what prayers they say; and, till they have learned them, makes them kneel by him: esteeming that this private praying is a more voluntary act in them than when they are called to others' prayers, and that which, when they leave the family, they carry with them. He keeps his servants between love and fear, according as he finds them. But, generally, he distributes it thus: to his children, he shews more love than terror; to his servants, more terror than love; but an old good servant boards a child.

The furniture of his house is very plain, but clean, whole, and sweet;—as sweet as his garden can make; for he hath no money for such things, charity being his only perfume, which deserves cost when he can spare it. His fare is plain, and common, but wholesome. What he hath is little, but very good. It consisteth most of mutton, beef, and veal; if he adds any thing for a great day or a stranger, his garden or orchard supplies it, or his barn, and backside. He goes no further for any entertainment, lest he go into the world; esteeming it absurd, that *he* should exceed, who teacheth others temperance. But those which his home produceth, he refuseth not; as coming cheap and easy, and arising from the improvement of things which otherwise would be lost. Wherein he admires and imitates the wonderful providence and thrift of the great Householder of the world. For, there being two things which, as they are, are unuseful to man,—the one for smallness, as crumbs and scattered corn, and the like; the other for the foulness, as wash, and dirt, and things thereinto fallen—God hath provided creatures for both: for the first, poultry; for the second, swine. These save man the labor; and, doing that which either he could not do, or was not fit for him to do, by taking both sorts of food into them, do as it were dress and prepare both for man in themselves, by growing themselves fit for his table.

The parson in his house observes fasting days. And particularly, as Sunday is his day of joy, so Friday his day of humiliation; which he celebrates not only with abstinence of diet, but also of company, recreation, and all outward contentments; and besides, with confession of sins, and all acts of mortification. Now fasting days contain a treble obligation: first, of eating less that day than on other days; secondly, of eating no pleasing or over-nourishing things, as the Israelites did eat sour herbs; thirdly, of eating no flesh—which is but the determination of the second rule, by authority, to this particular. The two former obligations are much more essential to a true fast, than the third and last; and fasting days were fully performed by keeping of the two former, had not authority interposed. So that to eat little, and that unpleasant, is the natural rule of fasting; although it be flesh. For, since fasting, in scripture language, is an afflicting of our souls, if a piece of dry flesh at my table be more unpleasant to me, than some fish there, certainly to eat the flesh, and not the fish, is to keep the fasting day naturally. And it is observable, that the prohibiting of flesh came from hot countries, where both flesh alone, and much more with wine, is apt to nourish more than in cold regions; and where flesh may be much better spared, and with more safety, than 'elsewhere, where (both the people and the drink being cold and phlegmatic) the eating of flesh is an antidote to both. For it is certain that a weak stomach being prepossessed with flesh, shall much better brook and bear a draught of beer, than if it had 'taken before either fish, or roots, or such things; which will discover itself by spitting, and rheum, or phlegm. To conclude, the parson, if he be in full health, keeps the three obligations; eating fish or roots; and *that*, for quantity little, for quality unpleasant. If his body be weak and obstructed, as most students are, he cannot keep the last obligation, nor suffer others in his house, that are so, to keep it: but only the two former; which also, in diseases of exinanition (as consumptions) must be broken: for meat was made for man, not man for meat. To all this may be added—not for the emboldening the unruly, but for the comfort of the weak—that not only sickness breaks these obligations of fasting, but sickliness also. For it is as unnatural to do any thing that leads me to a sickness to which I am inclined, as not to get out of that sickness when I am in it, by any diet. One thing is evident; that an English body, and a student's body, are two great obstructed vessels: and there is nothing that is food, and not physic, which doth less obstruct, than flesh moderately taken; as, being immoderately taken, it is exceeding obstructive. And obstructions are the cause of most diseases.

CHAPTER XI.
The Parson's Courtesy.

THE Country Parson owing a debt of charity to the poor, and of courtesy to his other parishioners, he so distinguisheth, that he keeps his money for the poor, and his table for those that are above alms. Not but that the poor are welcome also to his table; whom he sometimes purposely takes home with him, setting them close by him, and carving for them, both for his own humility, and their comfort, who are much cheered with such friendliness. But since both is to be done, the better sort invited, and meaner relieved, he chooseth rather to give the poor money; which they can better employ to their own advantage, and suitably to their needs, than so much given in meat at dinner. Having then invited some of his parish, he taketh his times to do the like to the rest; so that, in the compass of the year, he hath them all with him: because country people are very observant of such things; and will not be persuaded, but being not invited, they are hated. Which persuasion the parson by all means avoids; knowing that, where there are such conceits, there is no room for his doctrine to enter. Yet doth he oftenest invite those, whom he sees take best courses; that so both they may be encouraged to persevere, and others spurred to do well, that they may enjoy the like courtesy. For though he desire that all should live well and virtuously, not for any reward of his, but for virtue's sake: yet that will not be so. And therefore as God, although we should love him only for his own sake, yet out of his infinite pity hath set forth heaven for a reward to draw men to piety; and is content if, at least *so*, they will become good: so the country parson, who is a diligent observer and tracker of God's ways, sets up as many encouragements to goodness as he can, both in honor, and profit, and fame; that he may, if not the best way, yet *any* way, make his parish good.

CHAPTER XII.

The Parson's Charity.

THE Country Parson is full of charity; it is his predominant element. For many and wonderful things are spoken of thee, thou great virtue. To charity is given the covering of sins (1 Pet. iv. 8), and the forgiveness of sins (Matt. vi. 14, Luke vii. 47), the fulfilling of the law (Rom. xiii. 10), the life of faith (Jam. ii. 16), the blessings of this life (Prov. xxii. 9, Ps. xli. 2), and the reward of the next (Matt. xxv. 35). In brief, it is the body of religion (John xii. 35), and the top of Christian virtues (1 Cor. xiii.). Wherefore all his works relish of charity. When he riseth in the morning, he bethinketh himself what good deeds he can do that day, and presently doth them; counting that day lost, wherein he hath not exercised his charity.

He first considers his own parish; and takes care, that there be not a beggar or idle person in his parish, but that all be in a competent way of getting their living. This he effects either by bounty, or persuasion, or by authority; making use of that excellent statute, which binds all parishes to maintain their own. If his parish be rich, he exacts this of them; if poor, and he able, he easeth them therein. But he gives no set pension to any; for this in time will lose the name and effect of charity with the poor people, though not with God; for then they will reckon upon it, as on a debt; and if it be taken away, though justly, they will murmur and repine as much, as he that is disseised of his own inheritance. But the parson, having a double aim, and making a hook of his charity, causeth them still to depend on him: and so, by continual and fresh bounties, unexpected to them but resolved to himself, he wins them to praise God more, to live more religiously, and to take more pains in their vocation, as not knowing when they shall be relieved; which otherwise they would reckon upon, and turn to idleness. Besides this general provision, he hath other times of opening his hand; as at great festivals and communions; not suffering any, that day that he receives, to want a good meal suiting to the joy of the occasion. But specially at hard times and dearths, he even parts his living and life among them; giving some corn outright, and selling other at under rates; and, when his own stock serves not, working those that are able to the same charity, still pressing it, in the pulpit and out of the pulpit, and never leaving them till he obtain his desire. Yet, in all his charity, he distinguisheth; giving them most who live best, and take most pains, and are most charged: so is his charity in effect a sermon.

After the consideration of his own parish, he enlargeth himself, if he be able, to the neighborhood; for that also is some kind of obligation. So doth he also to those at his door; whom God puts in his way, and makes his neighbors. But these he helps not without some testimony, except the evidence of the misery bring testimony with it. For though these testimonies also may be falsified, yet—considering that the law allows these in case they be true, but allows by no means to give without testimony—as he obeys authority in the one, so, *that* being once satisfied, he allows his charity some blindness in the other; especially since, of the two commands, we are more enjoined to be charitable than wise. But evident miseries have a natural privilege and exemption from all law. Whenever he gives any thing, and sees them labor in thanking of him, he exacts of them to let him alone, and say rather, "God be praised! God be glorified!" that so the thanks may go the right way, and thither only, where they are only due. So doth he also, before giving, make them say their prayers first, or the creed, and ten commandments; and, as he finds them perfect, rewards them the more. For other givings are lay and secular; but this is to give like a priest.

CHAPTER XIII.

The Parson's Church.

THE Country Parson hath a special care of his church, that all things there be decent, and befitting His name by which it is called. Therefore, First, he takes order, that all things be in good repair; as walls plastered, windows glazed, floor paved, seats whole, firm, and uniform, especially that the pulpit, and desk, and communion table, and font be as they ought, for those great duties that are performed in them. Secondly, that the church be swept, and kept clean, without dust or cobwebs; and, at great festivals, strewed and stuck with boughs, and perfumed with incense. Thirdly, that there be fit and proper texts of scripture every where painted; and that all the paintings be grave and reverend, not with light colors or foolish antics. Fourthly, that all the books appointed by authority be there; and those not torn or fouled, but whole and clean, and well bound : and that there be a fitting and sightly communion cloth of fine linen, with a handsome and seemly carpet of good and costly stuff or cloth, and all kept sweet and clean in a strong and decent chest; with a chalice and cover, and a stoop or flagon; and a bason for alms and offerings: besides which, he hath a poor man's box conveniently seated, to receive the charity of well-minded people, and to lay up treasure for the sick and needy.

And all this he doth, not as out of necessity, or as putting a holiness in the things, but as desirous to keep the middle way between superstition and slovenliness; and as following the apostle's two great and admirable rules in things of this nature; the first whereof is, *Let all things be done decently and in order:* the second, *Let all things be done to edification* (1 Cor. xiv.). For these two rules comprise and include the double object of our duty, God and our neighbor; the first being for the honor of God, the second for the benefit of our neighbor. So that they excellently score out the way, and full and exactly contain, even in external and indifferent things, what course is to be taken; and put them to great shame, who deny the scripture to be perfect.

CHAPTER XIV.

The Parson in Circuit.

The Country Parson, upon the afternoons in the week-days, takes occasion sometimes to visit in person, now one quarter of his parish, now another. For there he shall find his flock most naturally as they are, wallowing in the midst of their affairs; whereas on Sundays it is easy for them to compose themselves to order, which they put on as their holiday clothes, and come to church in frame, but commonly the next day put off both.

When he comes to any house, first he blesseth it; and then, as he finds the persons of the house employed, so he forms his discourse.—Those that he finds religiously employed, he both commends them much, and furthers them, when he is gone, in their employment: as, if he finds them reading, he furnisheth them with good books; if curing poor people, he supplies them with receipts, and instructs them further in that skill, shewing them how acceptable such works are to God, and wishing them ever to do the cures with their own hands, and not to put them over to servants.

Those that he finds busy in the works of their calling, he commendeth them also: for if is a good and just thing for every one to do their own business. But then he admonisheth them of two things—First, that they dive not too deep into worldly affairs, plunging themselves over head and ears into carking and caring; but that they so labor, as neither to labor anxiously, nor distrustfully, nor profanely. (Then they labor anxiously, when they overdo it, to the loss of their quiet and health. Then distrustfully, when they doubt God's providence, thinking that their own labor is the cause of their thriving, as if it were in their own hands to thrive or not to thrive. Then they labor profanely, when they set themselves to work like brute beasts, never raising their thoughts to God, nor sanctifying their labor with daily prayer: when on the Lord's day they do unnecessary servile work, or in time of divine service on other holy days; except in the cases of extreme poverty, and in the seasons of seed time and harvest.) Secondly, he adviseth them so to labor for wealth and maintenance, as that they make not that the end of their labor; but that they may have wherewithal to serve God the better, and do good deeds. After these discourses, if they be poor and needy whom he thus finds laboring, he gives them somewhat; and opens not only his mouth, but his purse to their relief, that so they go on more cheerfully in their vocation, and himself be ever the more welcome to them.

Those that the parson finds idle or ill employed, he chides not at first, for that were neither civil nor profitable; but always in the close, before he departs from them. Yet in this he distinguisheth. For if he be a plain countryman, he reproves him plainly; for they are not sensible of fineness. If they be of higher quality, they commonly are quick, and sensible, and very tender of reproof; and therefore he lays his discourse so, that he comes to the point very leisurely; and oftentimes, as Nathan did, in the person of another making them to reprove themselves. However, one way or other, he ever reproves them, that he may keep himself pure, and not be entangled in others' sins. Neither in this doth he forbear, though there be company by. For as, when the offence is particular, and against *me*, I am to follow our Saviour's rule, and to take my brother aside and reprove him; so, when the offence is public, and against God, I am then to follow the apostle's rule (I Tim. v. 20), and to *rebuke openly* that which is done openly.

Besides these occasional discourses, the parson questions what order is kept in the house; as about prayers morning and evening on their knees, reading of scripture, catechising, singing of psalms at their work and on holidays,—who can read, who not: and sometimes he hears the children read himself, and blesseth them; encouraging also the servants to learn to read, and offering to have them taught on holidays by his servants. If the parson were ashamed of particularizing in these things, he were not fit to be a parson. But he holds the rule, that nothing is little in God's service: if it once have the honor of THAT NAME, it grows great instantly. Wherefore, neither disdaineth he to enter into the poorest cottage, though he even creep into it, and though it smell never so loathsomely. For both God is there also, and those for whom God died. And so much the rather doth he so, as his access to the poor is more comfortable, than to the rich; and, in regard of himself, it is more humiliation.

These are the parson's general aims in his circuit; but with these he mingles other discourses for conversation sake, and to make his higher purposes slip the more easily.

CHAPTER XV.

The Parson Comforting.

The Country Parson, when any of his cure is sick, or afflicted with loss of friend or estate, or any ways distressed, fails not to afford his best comforts: and rather goes to them, than sends for the afflicted; though they can, and otherwise ought to come to him. To this end he hath thoroughly digested all the points of consolation, as having continual use of them: such as are from God's *general* providence, extended even to lilies;—from his *particular*, to his church;—from his promises;—from the examples of all saints that ever were;—from Christ himself, perfecting our redemption no other way than by sorrow;—from the benefit of affliction, which softens and works the stubborn heart of man;—from the certainty both of deliverance and reward, if we faint not;—from the miserable comparison of the moment of griefs here, with the weight of joys hereafter. Besides this, in his visiting the sick or otherwise afflicted, he followeth the church's counsel, namely, in persuading them to particular confession; laboring to make them understand the great good use of this ancient and pious ordinance, and how necessary it is in some cases. He also urgeth them to do some pious charitable works, as a necessary evidence and fruit of their faith, at that time especially. The participation of the holy sacrament,—how comfortable and sovereign a medicine it is to all sin-sick souls; what strength, and joy, and peace it administers against all temptations, even to death itself—he plainly and *generally* intimateth to the disaffected or sick person; that so the hunger and thirst after it may come rather from themselves, than from his persuasion.

CHAPTER XVI.

The Parson a Father.

THE Country Parson is not only a father to his flock, but also professes himself throughly of the opinion, carrying it about with him as full, as if he had begot his whole parish. And of this he makes great use. For by this means, when any sins, he hateth him not as an officer, but pities him as a father. And even in those wrongs which either in tithing or otherwise are done to his own person, he considers the offender as a child; and forgives, so he may have any sign of amendment. So also when, after many admonitions, any continue to be refractory, yet he gives him not over, but is long before he proceed to disinheriting: or perhaps never goes so far, knowing that some are called at the eleventh hour; and therefore he still expects and waits, lest he should determine God's hour of coming; which, as he cannot, touching the last day, so neither touching the intermediate days of conversion.

CHAPTER XVII.

The Parson in Journey.

THE Country Parson, when a just occasion calleth him out of his parish (which he diligently and strictly weigheth, his parish being all his joy and thought), leaveth not his ministry behind him; but is himself wherever he is. Therefore those he meets on the way he blesseth audibly: and with those he overtakes, or that overtake him, he begins good discourses, such as may edify; interposing sometimes some short and honest refreshments, which may make his other discourses more welcome, and less tedious. And when he comes to his inn, he refuseth not to join, that he may enlarge the glory of God to the company he is in, by a due blessing of God for their safe arrival, and saying grace at meat: and at going to bed, by giving the host notice, that he will have prayers in the hall, wishing him to inform his guests thereof, that if any be willing to partake, they may resort thither. The like he doth in the morning: using pleasantly the outlandish proverb, that " Prayers and provender never hinder journey." When he comes to any other house, where his kindred or other relations give him any authority over the family, if he be to stay for a time, he considers diligently the state thereof to God-ward; and that in two points: First, what disorders there are either in apparel, or diet, or too open a buttery, or reading vain books, or swearing, or breeding up children to no calling, but in idleness, or the like. Secondly, what means of piety, whether daily prayers be used, grace, reading of scriptures, and other good books; how Sundays, holidays, and fasting days are kept. And, accordingly as he finds any defect in these, he first considers with himself what kind of remedy fits the temper of the house best, and then he faithfully and boldly supplieth it; yet seasonable and discreetly, by taking aside the lord or lady, or master and mistress of the house, and shewing them clearly, that *they* respect them most who wish them best, and that not a desire to meddle with others' affairs, but the earnestness to do all the good he can, moves him to say thus and thus.

CHAPTER XVIII.

The Parson in Sentinel.

THE Country Parson, wherever he is, keeps God's watch; that is, there is nothing spoken or done in the company where he is, but comes under his test and censure. If it be well spoken or done, he takes occasion to commend and enlarge it; if ill, he presently lays hold of it, lest the poison steal into some young and unwary spirits, and possess them even before they themselves heed it. But this he doth discreetly, with mollifying and suppling words;—"this is not so well said, as it might have been forborne;"—"we cannot allow this." Or else, if the thing will admit interpretation,—"your meaning is not thus, but thus;"—or, "so far indeed what you say is true, and well said; but *this* will not stand." This is called keeping God's watch, when the baits which the enemy lays in company are discovered and avoided. This is to be on God's side, and be true to his party. Besides, if he perceive in company any discourse tending to ill, either by the wickedness or quarrelsomeness thereof, he either prevents it judiciously, or breaks it off seasonably by some diversion. Wherein a pleasantness of disposition is of great use, men being willing to sell the interest and engagement of their discourses for no price sooner than that of mirth; whither the nature of man, loving refreshment, gladly betakes itself, even to the loss of honor

CHAPTER XIX

The Parson in Reference.

THE Country Parson is sincere and upright in all his relations. And, First, he is just to his country; as when he is set at an armor or horse, he borrows them not to serve the turn, nor provides slight and unuseful, but such as are every way fitting to do his country true and laudable service, when occasion requires. To do otherwise, is deceit: and therefore not for him who is hearty and true in all his ways, as being the servant of Him in whom there was no guile. Likewise in any other country duty, he considers what is the end of any command, and then he suits things faithfully according to that end.—Secondly, he carries himself very respectfully, as to all the fathers of the church, so especially to his diocesan, honoring him both in word and behavior, and resorting unto him in any difficulty, either in his studies or in his parish. He observes visitations; and, being there, makes due use of them, as of clergy councils for the benefit of the diocese. And therefore, before he comes having observed some defects in the ministry, he then either in sermon, if he preach, or at some other time of the day, propounds among his brethren what were fitting to be done.—Thirdly, he keeps good correspondence with all the neighboring pastors round about him, performing for them any ministerial office, which is not to the prejudice of his own parish. Likewise he welcomes to his house any minister, how poor or mean soever, with as joyful a countenance, as if he were to entertain some great lord.—Fourthly, he fulfils the duty and debt of neighborhood, to all the parishes which are near him. For, the apostle's rule (Phil. iv.) being admirable and large, that we should do *whatsoever things are honest, or just, or pure, or lovely, or of good report, if there be any virtue, or any praise;* and neighborhood being ever reputed, even among the heathen, as an obligation to do good, rather than to those that are further, where things are otherwise equal; therefore he satisfies this duty also. Especially, if God have sent any calamity, either by fire or famine, to any neighboring parish, then he expects no brief, but taking his parish together the next Sunday or holy-day, and exposing to them the uncertainty of human affairs, none knowing whose turn may be next, and then, when he hath affrighted them with this, exposing the obligation of charity and neighborhood, he first gives himself liberally, and then incites them to give; making together a sum either to be sent, or, which were more comfortable, all together choosing some fit day to carry it themselves, and cheer the afflicted. So, if any neighboring village be overburdened with poor, and his own less charged, he finds some way of relieving it, and reducing the manna and bread of charity to some equality; representing to his people, that the blessing of God to them ought to make them the more charitable, and not the less, lest he cast their neighbors' poverty on them also.

CHAPTER XX.

The Parson in God's Stead.

THE Country Parson is in God's stead to his parish, and dischargeth God what he can of his promises. Wherefore there is nothing done either well or ill, whereof he is not the rewarder or punisher. If he chance to find any reading in another's bible, he provides him one of his own. If he find another giving a poor man a penny, he gives him a tester for it, if the giver be fit to receive it; or if he be of a condition above such gifts, he sends him a good book, or easeth him in his tithes, telling him, when he hath forgotten it, "This I do, because at such and such a time you were charitable. This is in some sort a discharging of God as concerning this life, who hath promised that godliness shall be gainful: but in the other, God is his own immediate pay-master, rewarding all good deeds to their full proportion. The parson's punishing of sin and vice, is rather by withdrawing his bounty and courtesy from the parties offending, or by private or public reproof, as the case requires, than by causing them to be presented or otherwise complained of. And yet as the malice of the person, or heinousness of the crime may be, he is careful to see condign punishment inflicted, and with truly godly zeal, without hatred to the person, hungereth and thirsteth after righteous punishment of unrighteousness.—Thus both in rewarding virtue, and in punishing vice, the parson endeavoreth to be in God's stead: knowing that country people are drawn or led by sense, more than by faith; by present rewards or punishments, more than by future.

CHAPTER XXI.

The Parson Catechising.

THE Country Parson values catechising highly. For, there being three points of his duty—the one, to infuse a competent knowledge of salvation in every one of his flock; the other, to multiply and build up this knowledge to a spiritual temple; the third, to inflame this knowledge, to press and drive it to practice, turning it to reformation of life, by pithy and lively exhortations; —catechising is the first point, and, but by catechising, the other cannot be attained. Besides, whereas in sermons there is a kind of state, in catechising there is a humbleness very suitable to Christian regeneration; which exceedingly delights him, as by way of exercise upon himself, and by way of preaching to himself, for the advancing of his own mortification; for in preaching to others, he forgets not himself, but is first a sermon to himself, and then to others; growing with the growth of his parish.

He useth and preferreth the ordinary church catechism; partly for obedience to authority, partly for uniformity sake, that the same common truths may be every where professed; especially since many remove from parish to parish, who like Christian soldiers are to give the word, and to satisfy the congregation by their catholic answers.—He exacts of all the doctrine of the catechism; of the younger sort, the very words; of the elder, the substance. Those he catechiseth publicly; these privately, giving age honor, according to the apostle's rule (1 Tim. v. 1).—He requires all to be present at catechising: first, for the authority of the work; secondly, that parents and masters, as they hear the answers prove, may when they come home either commend or reprove, either reward or punish; thirdly, that those of the elder sort, who are not well grounded, may then by an honorable way take occasion to be better instructed; fourthly, that those who are well grown in the knowledge of religion, may examine their grounds, renew their vows, and, by occasion of both, enlarge their meditations.

When once all have learned the words of the catechism, he thinks it the most useful way that a pastor can take, to go over the same, but in other words; for many say the catechism by rote, as parrots, without ever piercing into the sense of it. In this course the order of the catechism would be kept, but the rest varied; as thus. In the creed—" How came this world to be as it is? Was it made, or came it by chance? Who made it? Did you see God make it? Then are there some things to be believed that are not seen? Is this the nature of belief? Is not Christianity full of such things as are not to be seen, but believed?—You said God made the world; who is God?"—and so forward, requiring answers to all these; and helping and cherishing the answerer, by making the question very plain with comparisons; and making much even of a word of truth from him. This order, being used to one, would be a little varied to another. And this is an admirable way of teaching, wherein the catechised will at length find delight; and by which the catechiser, if he once get the skill of it, will draw out of ignorant and silly souls even the dark and deep points of religion. Socrates did thus in philosophy, who held that the seeds of all truths lay in every body; and accordingly, by questions well ordered, he found philosophy in silly tradesmen. That position will not hold in Christianity, because it contains things above nature; but after that the catechism is once learned, that which nature is towards philosophy, the catechism is towards divinity. To this purpose, some dialogues in Plato were worth the reading, where the singular dexterity of Socrates in this kind may be observed and imitated.—Yet the skill consists but in these three points:—First, an aim and mark of the whole discourse, whither to drive the answerer (which the questionist must have in his mind before any question be propounded) upon which and to which the questions are to be chained. Secondly, a most plain and easy framing the question even containing in virtue the answer also, especially to the more ignorant. Thirdly, when the answerer sticks, an illustrating the thing by something else, which he knows; making what he knows to serve him in that which he knows not. As when the parson once demanded, after other questions about man's misery, "Since man is so miserable, what is to be done?" and the answerer could not tell: he asked him again, what he would do if he were in a ditch. This familiar illustration made the answer so plain, that he was even ashamed of his ignorance; for he could not but say, he would haste out of it as fast as he could. Then he proceeded to ask, whether he could get out of the ditch alone, or whether he needed a helper, and who was that helper.—This is the skill, and doubtless the holy scripture intends thus much, when it condescends to the naming of a plough, a hatchet, a bushel, leaven, boys piping and dancing; shewing that things of ordinary use are not only to serve in the way of drudgery, but to be washed and cleansed, and serve for lights even of heavenly truths. This is the practice which the parson so much commends to all his fellow-laborers; the secret of whose good consists in this, that at sermons and prayers men may sleep or wander; but when one is asked a question, he must discover what he is. This practice exceeds even sermons in teaching: but, there being two things in sermons, the one informing, the other inflaming; as sermons come short of questions in the one, so they far exceed them in the other. For questions cannot inflame or ravish; that must be done by a set, and labored, and continued speech.

CHAPTER XXII.

The Parson in Sacraments.

THE Country Parson, being to administer the sacraments, is at a stand with himself, how or what behavior to assume for so holy things. Especially at communion times he is in a great confusion, as being not only to receive God, but to break and administer him. Neither finds he any issue in this, but to throw himself down at the throne of grace, saying, "Lord, thou knowest what thou didst, when thou appointedst it to be done thus; therefore do thou fulfil what thou didst appoint: for thou art not only the feast, but the way to it."

At baptism, being himself in white, he requires the presence of all, and baptizeth not willingly, but on Sundays or great days. He admits no vain or idle names, but such as are usual and accustomed. He says that prayer with great devotion, where God is thanked for calling us to the knowledge of his grace; baptism being a blessing, that the world hath not the like. He willingly and cheerfully crosseth the child; and thinketh the ceremony not only innocent, but reverend. He instructeth the godfathers and godmothers, that it is no complimental or light thing to sustain that place, but a great honor, and no less burden; as being done both in the presence of God and his saints, and by way of undertaking for a Christian soul. He adviseth all to call to mind their baptism often. For if wise men have thought it the best way of preserving a state, to reduce it to its principles by which it grew great; certainly it is the safest course for Christians also to meditate on their baptism often (being the first step into their great and glorious calling), and upon what terms, and with what vows they were baptized.

At the times of the holy communion, he first takes order with the church wardens, that the elements be of the best; not cheap, or coarse; much less ill-tasted, or unwholesome.—Secondly, he considers and looks into the ignorance or carelessness of his flock, and accordingly applies himself with catechisings and lively exhortations, not on the Sunday of the communion only (for then it is too late), but the Sunday, or Sundays, before the communion; or on the eves of all those days. If there be any who, having not received yet, are to enter into this great work, he takes the more pains with them, that he may lay the foundation of future blessings. The time of every one's first receiving is not so much by years, as by understanding. Particularly the rule may be this:—When any one can distinguish the sacramental from common bread, knowing the institution and the difference, he ought to receive, of what age soever. Children and youth are usually deferred too long, under pretence of devotion to the sacrament; but it is for want of instruction: their understandings being ripe enough for ill things, and why not then for better? But parents and masters should make haste in this, as to a great purchase for their children and servants: which while they defer both sides suffer; the one, in wanting many excitings of grace; the other, in being worse served and obeyed. The saying of the catechism is necessary, but not enough: because to answer in form may still admit ignorance. But the questions must be propounded loosely and widely, and then the answerer will discover what he is.—Thirdly, for the manner of receiving, as the parson useth all reverence himself, so he administers to none but to the reverent. The feast indeed requires sitting because it is a feast; but man's unpreparedness asks kneeling. He that comes to the sacrament hath the confidence of a guest; and he that kneels, confesseth himself an unworthy one, and therefore differs from other feasters; but he that sits, or lies, puts up to an apostle. Contentiousness in a feast of charity is more scandal than any posture.—Fourthly, touching the frequency of the communion, the parson celebrates it, if not duly once a month, yet at least five or six times in the year; as, at Easter, Christmas, Whitsuntide, afore and after harvest, and the beginning of Lent. And this he doth, not only for the benefit of the work, but also for the discharge of the church wardens; who being to present all who receive not thrice a year, if there be but three communions, neither can all the people so order their affairs as to receive just at those times, nor the church wardens so well take notice, who receive thrice, and who not.

CHAPTER XXIII.

The Parson's Completeness.

The Country Parson desires to be all to his parish; and not only a pastor, but a lawyer also, and a physician. Therefore he endures not that any of his flock should go to law; but, in any controversy, that they should resort to him as their judge. To this end, he hath gotten to himself some insight in things ordinarily incident and controverted, by experience, and by reading some initiatory treatises in the law, with Dalton's Justice of Peace, and the abridgments of the Statutes; as also by discourse with men of that profession, whom he hath ever some cases to ask, when he meets with them; holding that rule, that to put men to discourse of that wherein they are most eminent, is the most gainful way of conversation. Yet whenever any controversy is brought to him, he never decides it alone, but sends for three or four of the ablest of the parish to hear the cause with him, whom he makes to deliver their opinion first; out of which he gathers, in case he be ignorant himself, what to hold: and so the thing passeth with more authority and less envy. In judging, he follows that which is altogether right; so that if the poorest man of the parish detain but a pin unjustly from the richest, he absolutely restores it as a judge; but when he hath so done, then he assumes the parson, and exhorts to charity. Nevertheless, there may happen sometimes some cases, wherein he chooseth to permit his parishioners rather to make use of the law, than himself: as in cases of an obscure and dark nature, not easily determinable by lawyers themselves; or in cases of any consequence, as establishing of inheritances; or lastly, when the persons in difference are of a contentious disposition, and cannot be gained, but that they still fall from all compromises that have been made. But then he shews them how to go to law, even as brethren, and not as enemies, neither avoiding therefore one another's company, much less defaming one another.

Now as the parson is in law, so is he in sickness also. If there be any of his flock sick, he is their physician,— or at least his wife; of whom, instead of the qualities of the world, he asks no other, but to have the skill of healing a wound, or helping the sick. But if neither himself nor his wife have the skill, and his means serve, he keeps some young practitioner in his house for the benefit of his parish; whom yet he ever exhorts not to exceed his bounds, but in tickle cases to call in help. If all fail, then he keeps good correspondence with some neighbor physician, and entertains him for the cure of his parish. Yet it is easy for any scholar to attain to such a measure of physic, as may be of much use to him, both for himself and others. This is done by seeing one anatomy, reading one book of physic, having one herbal by him. And let Fernelius be the physic author, for he writes briefly, neatly, and judiciously; especially let his Method of physic be diligently perused, as being the practical part, and of most use. Now both the reading of him and the knowing of herbs may be done at such times, as they may be a help and a recreation to more divine studies, nature serving grace both in comfort of diversion, and the benefit of application when need requires it; as also by way of illustration, even as our Saviour made plants and seeds to teach the people. For he was the true *householder, who bringeth out of his treasury things new and old,*—the old things of philosophy, and the new of grace; and maketh the one serve the other. And, I conceive, our Saviour did this for three reasons. First, that by familiar things he might make his doctrine slip the more easily into the hearts even of the meanest. Secondly, that laboring people, whom he chiefly considered, might have every where monuments of his doctrine; remembering, in gardens, his mustard-seed and lilies; in the field, his seed corn and tares: and so not be drowned altogether in the works of their vocation, but sometimes lift up their minds to better things, even in the midst of their pains. Thirdly, that he might set a copy for parsons.—In the knowledge of simples, wherein the manifold wisdom of God is wonderfully to be seen, one thing would be carefully observed; which is, to know what herbs may be used instead of drugs of the same nature, and to make the garden the shop. For home-bred medicines are both more easy for the parson's purse, and more familiar for all men's bodies. So, where the apothecary useth, either for loosing, rhubarb; or for binding, bolearmena; the parson useth damask or white roses for the one, and plaintain, shepherds-purse, knotgrass, for the other; and that with better success. As for spices, he doth not only prefer home-bred things before them, but condemns them for vanities, and so shuts them out of his family; esteeming that there is no spice comparable, for herbs, to rosemary, thyme, savory, mints; and for seeds, to fennel, and carraway-seeds. Accordingly for salves, his wife seeks not the city, but prefers her garden and fields before all outlandish gums. And surely hyssop, valerian, mercury, adders-tongue, yerrow, melilot, and St. John's-wort made into a salve; and elder, camomile, mallows, comphrey, and smallage made into a poultice, have done great and rare cures. In curing of any, the parson and his family use to premise prayers; for this is to cure like a parson, and this raiseth the action from the shop to the church.—But though the parson sets forward all charitable deeds, yet he looks not in this point of curing beyond his own parish; except the person be so poor, that he is not able to reward the physician. For, as he is charitable, so he is just also. Now it is a justice and debt to the commonwealth he lives in, not to encroach on others' professions, but to live on his own. And justice is the ground of charity.

CHAPTER XXIV.

The Parson Arguing.

THE Country Parson, if there be any of his parish that hold strange doctrines, useth all possible diligence to reduce them to the common faith.—The first means he useth is prayer; beseeching the Father of lights to open their eyes, and to give him power so to fit his discourse to them, that it may effectually pierce their hearts, and convert them.—The second means is a very loving and sweet usage of them, both in going to, and sending for them often, and in finding out courtesies to place on them; as in their tithes, or otherwise.—The third means is the observation what is the main foundation and pillar of their cause, whereon they rely; as, if he be a papist, the church is the hinge he turns on; if a schismatic, scandal. Wherefore the parson hath diligently examined these two with himself. As, what the church is; how it begun; how it proceeded; whether it be a rule to itself; whether it hath a rule; whether, having a rule, it ought not to be guided by it; whether any rule in the world be obscure; and how then should the best be so? at least in fundamental things;—the obscurity in some points being the exercise of the church, the light in the foundations being the guide;—the church needing both an evidence and an exercise. So, for scandal: what scandal is; when given or taken; whether, there being two precepts, one of obeying authority, the other of not giving scandal, *that* ought not to be preferred,—especially since in disobeying there is scandal also; whether, things once indifferent, being made by the precept of authority more than indifferent, it be in our power to omit or refuse them. These and the like points he hath accurately digested; having ever, besides, two great helps and powerful persuaders on his side. The one, a strict religious life; the other, a humble and ingenuous search of truth, being unmoved in arguing, and void of all contentiousness: which are two great lights able to dazzle the eyes of the misled, while they consider, that God cannot be wanting to them in doctrine, to whom he is so gracious in life.

CHAPTER XXV.

The Parson Punishing.

WHENSOEVER the Country Parson proceeds so far as to call in authority, and to do such things of legal opposition, either in the presenting or punishing of any, as the vulgar ever construes for signs of ill will, he forbears not in any wise to use the delinquent as before, in his behavior and carriage towards him, not avoiding his company, or doing any thing of averseness, save in the very act of punishment. Neither doth he esteem him for an enemy, but as a brother still; except some small and temporary estranging may corroborate the punishment to a better subduing and humbling of the delinquent. Which, if it happily take effect, he then comes on the faster, and makes so much the more of him, as before he alienated himself; doubling his regards, and shewing, by all means, that the delinquent's return is to his advantage.

CHAPTER XXVI.

The Parson's Eye.

THE Country Parson, at spare times from action, standing on a hill and considering his flock, discovers two sorts of vices, and two sorts of vicious persons. There are some vices, whose natures are always clear and evident; as adultery, murder, hatred, lying, &c. There are other vices, whose natures, at least in the beginning, are dark and obscure; as coveteousness, and gluttony. So likewise there are some persons, who abstain not even from known sins: there are others, who when they know a sin evidently, they commit it not. It is true indeed, they are long a knowing it, being partial to themselves, and witty to others who shall reprove them for it. A man may be both covetous and intemperate, and yet hear sermons against both, and himself condemn both in good earnest. And the reason hereof is, because, the natures of these vices being not evidently discussed or known commonly, the beginnings of them are not easily observable: and the beginnings of them are not observed, because of the sudden passing from that which was just now lawful, to that which is presently unlawful even in one continued action. So, a man dining eats at first lawfully: but, proceeding on, comes to do unlawfully, even before he is aware; not knowing the bounds of the action, nor when his eating begins to be unlawful. So, a man storing up money for his necessary provisions, both in present for his family and in future for his children, hardly perceives when his storing becomes unlawful: yet is there a period for his storing, and a point or centre when his storing, which was even now good, passeth from good to bad.—Wherefore the parson, being true to his business, hath exactly sifted the definitions of all virtue and vices; especially canvassing those, whose natures are most stealing, and beginnings uncertain. Particularly, concerning these two vices; not because they are all that are of this dark and creeping disposition, but for example sake, and because they are most common; he thus thinks:—

First, for covetousness, he lays this ground. Whosoever, when a just occasion calls, either spends not at all, or not in some proportion to God's blessing upon him, is covetous. The reason of the ground is manifest; because wealth is given to that end, to supply our occasions. Now, if I do not give every thing its end, I abuse the creature; I am false to my reason, which should guide me; I offend the supreme Judge, in perverting that order which he hath set both to things and to reason. The application of the ground would be infinite. But, in brief, a poor man is an occasion; my country is an occasion; my friend is an occasion; my table is an occasion; my apparel is an occasion. If in all these, and those more which concern me, I either do nothing, or pinch, and scrape, and squeeze blood, undecently to the station wherein God hath placed me, I am covetous. More particularly, and to give one instance for all; if God have given me servants, and I either provide too little for them, or that which is unwholesome, being sometimes baned meat, sometimes too salt, and so not competent nourishment, I am covetous. I bring this example, because men usually think, that servants for their money are as other things that they buy; even as a piece of wood, which they may cut or hack, or throw into the fire; and, so they pay them their wages, all is well.—Nay, to descend yet more particularly; if a man hath wherewithal to buy a spade, and yet he chooseth rather to use his neighbor's and wear out that, he is covetous.—Nevertheless, few bring covetousness thus low, or consider it so narrowly; which yet ought to be done, since there is a justice in the least things, and for the least there shall be a judgment. Country people are full of these petty injustices, being cunning to make use of another, and spare themselves. And scholars ought to be diligent in the observation of these, and driving of their general school-rules ever to the smallest actions of life; which, while they dwell in their books, they will never find; but, being seated in the country, and doing their duty faithfully, they will soon discover; especially if they carry their eyes ever open, and fix them on their charge, and not on their preferment.

Secondly, for gluttony, the parson lays this ground. He that either for quantity eats more than his health or employments will bear, or for quality is liquorous after dainties, is a glutton;—as he that eats more than his estate will bear, is a prodigal; and he that eats offensively to the company, either in his order or length of eating, is scandalous and uncharitable. These three rules generally comprehend the faults of eating; and the truth of them needs no proof. So that men must eat, neither to the disturbance of their health, nor of their affairs (which, being over-burdened, or studying dainties too much, they cannot well despatch), nor of their estate, nor of their brethren. One act in these things is bad; but it is the custom and habit that names a glutton. Many think they are at more liberty than they are, as if they were masters of their health; and, so they will stand to the pain, all is well. But to eat to one's hurt comprehends, besides the hurt, an act against reason, because it is unnatural to hurt one's self; and this they are *not* masters of. Yet, of hurtful things, I am more bound to abstain from those, which by mine own experience I have found hurtful, than from those which by a common tradition and vulgar knowledge are reputed to be so.—That which is said of hurtful meats, extends to hurtful drinks also. As for the quantity, touching our employments, none must eat so as to disable themselves from a fit discharging either of divine duties, or duties of their calling. So that, if after dinner they are not fit (or unwieldy) either to pray or work, they are gluttons. Not that all must presently work after dinner. For they rather must *not* work, especially students, and those that are weakly. But that they must rise so, as that it is not meat or drink that hinders them from working. To guide them in this, there are three rules. First, the custom and knowledge of their own body, and what it can well digest. The second, the feeling of themselves in time of eating; which because it is deceitful (for one thinks in eating, that he can eat more, than afterwards he finds true). The third is the observation with what appetite they sit down. This last rule, joined with the first, never fails. For, knowing what one usually can well digest, and feeling when I go to meat in what disposition I am, either hungry or not; according as I feel myself, either I take my wonted proportion, or diminish of it. Yet physicians bid those that would live in health, not keep a uniform diet, but to feed variously; now more, now less. And Gerson, a spiritual man, wisheth all to incline rather to too much, than to too little; his reason is, because diseases of exinanition are more dangerous than diseases of repletion. But the parson distinguisheth according to his double aim; either of abstinence a moral virtue, or mortification a divine. When he deals with any that is heavy and carnal, he gives him those freer rules. But when he meets with a refined and heavenly disposition, he carries them higher, even sometimes to a forgetting of themselves; knowing that there is one who, when they forget, remembers for them. As when the people hungered and thirsted after our Saviour's doctrine, and tarried so long at it, that they would have fainted had they returned empty, he suffered it not; but rather made food miraculously, than suffered so good desires to miscarry.

CHAPTER XXVII.

The Parson in Mirth.

THE Country Parson is generally sad, because he knows nothing but the cross of Christ; his mind being defixed on it with those nails wherewith his Master was. Or, if he have any leisure to look off from thence, he meets continually with two most sad spectacles,—sin and misery; God dishonored every day, and man afflicted. Nevertheless, he sometimes refresheth himself, as knowing that nature will not bear everlasting droopings, and that pleasantness of disposition is a great key to do good: not only because all men shun the company of perpetual severity; but also for that, when they are in company, instructions seasoned with pleasantness both enter sooner, and root deeper. Wherefore he condescends to human frailties, both in himself and others; and intermingles some mirth in his discourses occasionally, according to the pulse of the hearer.

CHAPTER XXVIII.

The Parson in Contempt.

THE Country Parson knows well, that,—both for the general ignominy which is cast upon the profession, and much more for those rules which out of his choicest judgment he hath resolved to observe, and which are described in this book,—he must be despised. Because this hath been the portion of God his Master, and of God's saints his brethren; and this is foretold, that it shall be so still, until things be no more. Nevertheless, according to the apostle's rule, he endeavors that none shall despise him; especially in his own parish he suffers it not, to his utmost power, for that, where contempt is, there is no room for instruction. This he procures, First, by his holy and unblamable life; which carries a reverence with it, even above contempt. Secondly, by a courteous carriage and winning behavior. He that will be respected, must respect; doing kindnesses, but receiving none, at least of those who are apt to despise; for this argues a height and eminency of mind, which is not easily despised, except it degenerate to pride. Thirdly, by a bold and impartial reproof, even of the best in the parish, when occasion requires: for this may produce hatred in those that are reproved, but never contempt, either in them or others. Lastly, if the contempt shall proceed so far as to do any thing punishable by law, as contempt is apt to do if it be not thwarted, the parson, having a due respect both to the person and to the cause, referreth the whole matter to the examination and punishment of those which are in authority: that so, the sentence lighting upon one, the example may reach to all.

But if the contempt be not punishable by law; or, being so, the parson think it in his discretion either unfit or bootless to contend: then, when any despises him, he takes it either in a humble way, saying nothing at all; —or else in a slighting way, shewing that reproaches touch him no more than a stone thrown against heaven, where he is and lives;—or in a sad way, grieved at his own and others' sins, which continually break God's laws, and dishonor him with those mouths which he continually fills and feeds;—or else in a doctrinal way, saying to the contemner, "Alas, why do you thus? you hurt yourself, not me; he that throws a stone at another, hits himself;" and so, between gentle reasoning and pitying, he overcomes the evil;—or, lastly, in a triumphant way, being glad and joyful that he is made conformable to his Master, and, being in the world as *he* was, hath this undoubted pledge of his salvation. These are the five shields, wherewith the godly receive the darts of the wicked: leaving anger, and retorting, and revenge to the children of the world; whom another's ill mastereth, and leadeth captive, without any resistance, even in resistance, to the same destruction. For while they resist the person that reviles, they resist not the evil which takes hold of them, and is far the worse enemy.

CHAPTER XXIX.

The Parson with his Church Wardens.

THE Country Parson doth often, both publicly and privately, instruct his church wardens, what a great charge lies upon them; and that, indeed, the whole order and discipline of the parish is put into their hands. If himself reform any thing, it is out of the overflowing of his conscience; whereas they are to do it by command, and by oath. Neither hath the place its dignity from the ecclesiastical laws only: since even by the common statute law they are taken for a kind of corporation, as being persons enabled by that name to take moveable goods or chattels, and to sue and to be sued at the law concerning such goods, for the use and profit of their parish; and, by the same law, they are to levy penalties for negligence in resorting to church, or for disorderly carriage in time of divine service. Wherefore the parson suffers not the place to be vilified or debased, by being cast on the lower rank of people; but invites and urges the best unto it, shewing that they do not lose or go less, but gain, by it;—it being the greatest honor of this world, to do God and his chosen service; or, as David says, *to be even a door-keeper in the house of God.*—Now, the canons being the church wardens' rule, the parson adviseth them to read or hear them read often, as also the visitation articles, which are grounded upon the canons; that so they may know their duty and keep their oath the better. In which regard, considering the great consequence of their place, and more of their oath, he wisheth them by no means to spare any, though never so great; but if, after gentle and neighborly admonitions, they still persist in ill, to present them; yea, though they be tenants, or otherwise engaged to the delinquent: for their obligation to God and their own soul is above any temporal tie. "Do well and right, and let the world sink."

CHAPTER XXX.

The Parson's Consideration of Providence.

THE Country Parson,—considering the great aptness country people have to think that all things come by a kind of natural course; and that if they sow and soil their grounds, they must have corn; if they keep and fodder well their cattle, they must have milk, and calves,—labors to reduce them to see God's hand in all things; and to believe, that things are not set in such an inevitable order, but that God often changeth it according as he sees fit, either for reward or punishment. To this end he represents to his flock, that God hath and exerciseth a threefold power, in every thing which concerns man. The first is a sustaining power; the second, a governing power; the third, a spiritual power. By his *sustaining power*, he preserves and actuates every thing in his being. So that corn doth not grow by any other virtue, than by that which he continually supplies as the corn needs it; without which supply, the corn would instantly dry up, as a river would if the fountain were stopped. And it is observable, that, if any thing could presume of an inevitable course and constancy in its operations, certainly it should be either the sun in heaven, or the fire on earth; by reason of their fierce, strong, and violent natures. Yet when God pleased, the sun stood still, the fire burned not.—By God's *governing power*, he preserves and orders the references of things one to the other. So that, though the corn do grow, and be preserved in that act by his sustaining power, yet if he suit not other things to the growth (as seasons and weather, and other accidents), by his governing power, the fairest harvests come to nothing. And it is observable, that God delights to have men feel, and acknowledge, and reverence his power; and therefore he often overturns things, when they are thought past danger. That is his time of interposing. As when a merchant hath a ship come home, after many a storm which it hath escaped, he destroys it sometimes in the very haven: or, if the goods be housed, a fire hath broken forth and suddenly consumed them. Now this he doth, that men should perpetuate, and not break off, their acts of dependence; how fair soever the opportunities present themselves. So that if a farmer should depend upon God all the year, and, being ready to put hand to sickle, shall then secure himself, and think all cocksure; then God sends such weather, as lays the corn and destroys it. Or if he depend on God further, even till he imbarn his corn, and then think all sure; then God sends a fire, and consumes all that he hath. For that he ought not to break off, but to continue, his dependence on God; not only before the corn is inned, but after also; and, indeed, to depend and fear continually.—The third *power* is *spiritual*, by which God turns all outward blessings to inward advantages. So that if a farmer hath both a harvest, and that also well inned and imbarned, and continuing safe there; yet if God give him not grace to use and utter this well, all his advantages are to his loss. Better were his corn burnt, than not spiritually improved. And it is observable in this, how God's goodness strives with man's refractoriness. Man would sit down at *this* world; God bids him sell it, and purchase a better. Just as a father, who hath in his hand an apple, and a piece of gold under it; the child comes, and with pulling gets the apple out of his father's hand; his father bids him throw it away, and he will give him the gold for it; which the child utterly refusing, eats it, and is troubled with worms,—so is the carnal and wilful man with the worm of the grave in this world, and the worm of conscience in the next.

CHAPTER XXXI.

The Parson in Liberty.

THE Country Parson, observing the manifold wiles of Satan (who plays his part, sometimes in drawing God's servants from him, sometimes in perplexing them in the service of God), stands fast in the liberty wherewith Christ hath made us free. This liberty he compasseth by one distinction; and that is, of what is necessary, and what is additionary. As for example: it is necessary, that all Christians should pray twice a day, every day of the week, and four times on Sunday, if they be well. This is so necessary and essential to a Christian, that he cannot, without this, maintain himself in a Christian state. Besides this, the godly have ever added some hours of prayer; as at nine, or at three, or at midnight, or as they think fit, and see cause,—or, rather, as God's Spirit leads them. But these prayers are not necessary, but additionary. Now it so happens, that the godly petitioner, upon some emergent interruption in the day, or by oversleeping himself at night, omits his additionary prayer. Upon this, his mind begins to be perplexed and troubled; and Satan, who knows the exigent, blows the fire, endeavoring to disorder the Christian, and put him out of his station, and to enlarge the perplexity, until it spread, and taint his other duties of piety, which none can perform so well in trouble as in calmness. Here the parson interposeth with his distinction, and shews the perplexed Christian, that—this prayer being additionary, not necessary; taken in; not commanded,—the omission thereof upon just occasion ought by no means to trouble him. God knows the occasion as well as he; and he is as a gracious father, who more accepts a common course of devotion, than dislikes an occasional interruption. And of this he is so to assure himself, as to admit no scruple, but to go on as cheerfully as if he had not been interrupted. By this it is evident, that the distinction is of singular use and comfort; especially to pious minds, which are ever tender and delicate.—But here there are two cautions to be added. First, that this interruption proceed not out of slackness or coldness: which will appear if the pious soul foresee and prevent such interruptions, what he may, before they come; and when, for all that, they do come, he be a little affected therewith, but not afflicted or troubled; if he resent to a mislike, but not a grief. Secondly, that this interruption proceed not out of shame. As for example: a godly man, not out of superstition, but of reverence to God's house, resolves whenever he enters into a church, to kneel down and pray: either blessing God, that he will be pleased to dwell among men; or beseeching him that whenever he repairs to his house, he may behave himself so as befits so great a presence; and this briefly. But it happens that, near the place where he is to pray, he spies some scoffing ruffian, who is likely to deride him for his pains. If he now shall, either for fear or shame, break his custom, he shall do passing ill; so much the rather ought he to proceed, as that by this he may take into his prayer humiliation also. On the other side, if I am to visit the sick in haste, and my nearest way lie through the church, I will not doubt to go without staying to pray there (but only, as I pass, in my heart), because this kind of prayer is additionary, not necessary; and the other duty overweighs it; so that if any scruple arise, I will throw it away, and be most confident that God is not displeased.

This distinction may run through all Christian duties; and it is a great stay and settling to religious souls.

CHAPTER XXXII.

The Parson's Surveys.

THE Country Parson hath not only taken a particular survey of the faults of his own parish, but a general also of the diseases of the time; that so, when his occasions carry him abroad or bring strangers to him, he may be the better armed to encounter them.—The great and national sin of this land, he esteems to be idleness: great in itself, and great in consequence; for when men have nothing to do, then they fall to drink, to steal, to whore, to scoff, to revile, to all sorts of gamings.

"Come," say they, "we have nothing to do; let's go to the tavern, or to the stews;" or what not? Wherefore the parson strongly opposeth this sin, wheresoever he goes.

And because idleness is twofold,—the one in having no calling, the other in walking carelessly in our calling,—he first represents to every body the necessity of a vocation. The reason of this assertion is taken from the nature of man; wherein God hath placed two great instruments, reason in the soul, and a hand in the body, as engagements of working. So that even in paradise man had a calling; and how much more out of paradise? when the evils which he is now subject unto, may be prevented or diverted by reasonable employment. Besides, every gift or ability is a talent to be accounted for, and to be improved to our Master's advantage. Yet is it also a debt to our country to have a calling; and it concerns the commonwealth, that none should be idle, but all busied. Lastly, riches are the blessing of God, and the great instrument of doing admirable good; therefore all are to procure them, honestly and seasonably, when they are not better employed. Now this reason crosseth not our Saviour's precept of selling what we have; because, when we have sold all and given it to the poor, we must not be idle, but labor to get more, that we may give more; according to St. Paul's rule (Eph. iv. 28, 1 Thess. iv. 11, 12). So that our Saviour's selling is so far from crossing St. Paul's working, that it rather establisheth it; since they that have nothing, are fittest to work.

Now because the only opposer to this doctrine is the gallant, who is witty enough to abuse both others and himself, and who is ready to ask if he shall mend shoes, or what he shall do; therefore the parson, unmoved, sheweth, that ingenuous and fit employment is never wanting to those that seek it. But, if it should be, the assertion stands thus :—All are either to have a calling, or prepare for it: he that hath or can have yet no employment, if he truly and seriously prepare for it, he is safe, and within bounds. Wherefore all are either presently to enter into a calling, if they be fit for it, and it for them; or else to examine, with care and advice, what they are fittest for, and to prepare for that with all diligence.

But it will not be amiss, in this exceeding useful point, to descend to particulars; for exactness lies in particulars.

Men are either single, or married. The married and house-keeper hath his hands full, if he do what he ought to do. For there are two branches of his affairs: first, the improvement of his family, by bringing them up in the fear and nurture of the Lord; and secondly, the improvement of his grounds by drowning, or draining, stocking, or fencing, and ordering his land to the best advantage both of himself and his neighbors. The Italian says—" None fouls his hands in his own business." And it is an honest and just care, so it exceed not bounds, for every one to employ himself to the advancement of his affairs, that he may have wherewithal to do good. But his family is his best care: to labor Christian souls, and raise them to their height, even to heaven; to dress and prune them, and take as much joy in a straight-growing child or servant, as a gardener doth in a choice tree. Could men find out this delight, they would seldom be from home; whereas now, of any place, they are least there. But if, after all this care well despatched, the house-keeper's family be so small, and his dexterity so great, that he have leisure to look out, the village or parish which either he lives in, or is near unto it, is his employment. He considers every one there; and either helps them in particular, or hath general propositions to the whole town or hamlet, of advancing the public stock, and managing commons or woods, according as the place suggests. But if he may be of the commission of peace, there is nothing to that. No commonwealth in the world hath a better institution than that of justices of the peace. For it is both a security to the king, who hath so many dispersed officers at his beck throughout the kingdom, accountable for the public good; and also an honorable employment of a gentle or nobleman in the country he lives in, enabling him with power to do good, and to restrain all those who else might both trouble him and the whole state. Wherefore it behoves all, who are come to the gravity and ripeness of judgment for so excellent a place, not to refuse, but rather to procure it. And, whereas there are usually three objections made against the place :—the one, the abuse of it, by taking petty country bribes; the other, the casting of it on mean persons, especially in some shires; and lastly, the trouble of it: —these are so far from deterring any good man from the place, that they kindle them rather to redeem the dignity either from true faults, or unjust aspersions.

Now, for single men, they are either heirs, or younger brothers.—The heirs are to prepare in all the forementioned points against the time of their practice. Therefore they are to mark their father's discretion in ordering his house and affairs; and also elsewhere, when they see any remarkable point of education or good husbandry, and to transplant it in time to his own home; with the same care as others, when they meet with good fruit, get a graft of the tree, enriching their orchard, and neglecting their house. Besides, they are to read books of law and justice; especially the statutes at large. As for better books, of divinity, they are not in this consideration; because we are about a calling, and a preparation thereunto. But, chiefly and above all things, they are to frequent sessions and assizes. For it is both an honor which they owe to the reverend judges and magistrates, to attend them, at least in their shire: and it is a great advantage to know the practice of the land; for our law is practice. Sometimes he may go to court, as the eminent place both of good and ill. At other times he is to travel over the king's dominions; cutting out the kingdom into portions, which every year he surveys piecemeal. When there is a parliament, he is to endeavor by all means to be a knight or burgess there; for there is no school to a parliament. And when he is there, he must not only be a morning man, but at committees also; for there the particulars are exactly discussed, which are brought from thence to the house but in general. When none of these occasions call him abroad, every morning that he is at home he must either ride the great horse, or exercise some of his military gestures. For all gentlemen, that are not weakened and disarmed with sedentary lives, are to know the use of their arms; and as the husbandman labors for them, so must they fight for and defend him, when occasion calls. This is the duty of each to other, which they ought to fulfil; and the parson is a lover and exciter to justice in all things; even as John the Baptist squared out to every one, even to soldiers, what to do.—As for younger brothers, those whom the parson finds loose, and not engaged in some profession by their parents (whose neglect in this point is intolerable, and a shameful wrong both to the commonwealth and their own house), to them, after he hath shewed the unlawfulness of spending the day in dressing, complimenting, visiting, and sporting, he first commends the study of the civil law, as a brave and wise knowledge; the professors whereof were much employed by Queen Elizabeth; because it is the key of commerce, and discovers the rules of foreign nations. Secondly, he commends the mathematics, as the only wonder-working knowledge, and therefore requiring the best spirits. After the several knowledge of these, he adviseth to insist and dwell chiefly on the two noble branches thereof, of fortification and navigation; the one being useful to all countries, and the other especially to islands. But if the young gallant think these courses dull and phlegmatic, where can he busy himself better, than in those new plantations and discoveries, which are not only a noble, but also, as they may be handled, a religious employment? Or let him travel into Germany and France; and, observing the artifices and manufactures there, transplant them hither, as divers have done lately, to our country's advantage.

CHAPTER XXXIII.

The Parson's Library.

THE Country Parson's library is A HOLY LIFE; for (besides the blessing that that brings upon it,—there being a promise, that if the kingdom of God be first sought, all other things shall be added) even itself is a sermon. For, the temptations with which a good man is beset, and the ways which he used to overcome them, being told to another, whether in private conference or in the church, are a sermon. He that hath considered how to carry himself at table about his appetite, if he tell this to another, preacheth; and much more feelingly and judiciously, than he writes his rules of temperance out of books. So that the parson having studied and mastered all his lusts and affections within, and the whole army of temptations without, hath ever so many sermons ready penned, as he hath victories. And it fares in this as it doth in physic. He that hath been sick of a consumption, and knows what recovered him, is a physician, so far as he meets with the same disease and temper; and can much better and particulaly do it, than he that is generally learned, and was never sick. And if the same person had been sick of all diseases, and were recovered of all, by things that he knew, there were no such physician as he, both for skill and tenderness. Just so it is in divinity; and that not without manifest reason. For though the temptations may be diverse in divers Christians, yet the victory is alike in all, being by the selfsame Spirit.

Neither is this true only in the military state of a Christian life, but even in the peaceable also; when the servant of God, freed for a while from temptation, in a quiet sweetness seeks how to please his God. Thus the parson, considering that repentance is the great virtue of the gospel, and one of the first steps of pleasing God, having for his own use examined the nature of it, is able to explain it after to others. And, particularly, having doubted sometimes, whether his repentance were true, or at least in that degree it ought to be,—since he found himself sometimes to weep more for the loss of some temporal things, than for offending God,—he came at length to this resolution, that repentance is an act of the mind, not of the body (even as the original signifies), and that the chief thing which God in scriptures requires, is the heart and the spirit, and to worship him in truth and spirit. Wherefore, in case a Christian endeavor to weep and cannot, since we are not masters of our own bodies, this sufficeth. And consequently he found that the essence of repentance (that it may be alike in all God's children,—which, as concerning weeping, it cannot be, some being of a more melting temper than others) consisteth in a true detestation of the soul, abhorring and renouncing sin, and turning unto God in truth of heart and newness of life: which acts of repentance are and must be found in all God's servants. Not that weeping is not useful, where it can be (that so the body may join in the grief, as it did in the sin), but that, so the other acts be, *that* is not necessary. So that he as truly repents, who performs the other acts of repentance, when he cannot more, as he that weeps a flood of tears.—This instruction and comfort the parson getting for himself, when he tells it to others, becomes a sermon. The like he doth in other Christian virtues, as of faith, and love, and the cases of conscience belonging thereto; wherein (as St. Paul implies that he ought, Rom. ii.), he first preacheth to himself, and then to others.

CHAPTER XXXIV.

The Parson's Dexterity in Applying of Remedies.

THE Country Parson knows that there is a double state of a Christian even in this life; the one military, the other peaceable. The military is, when we are assaulted with temptations, either from within or from without. The peaceable is, when the devil for a time leaves us, as he did our Saviour, and the angels minister to us their own food, even joy, and peace, and comfort in the Holy Ghost. These two states were in our Saviour, not only in the beginning of his preaching, but afterwards also (as, Matt. xxii. 35, he was tempted; and Luke x. 21, he rejoiced in spirit): and they must be likewise in all that be his. Now the parson having a spiritual judgment, according as he discovers any of his flock to be in one and the other state, so he applies himself to them.

Those that he finds in the peaceable state, he adviseth to be very vigilant, and not to let go the reins as soon as the horse goes easy. Particularly, he counselleth them to two things. First, to take heed lest their quiet betray them, as it is apt to do, to a coldness and carelessness in their devotions; but to labor still to be as fervent in Christian duties, as they remember themselves were, when affliction did blow the coals. Secondly, not to take the full compass and liberty of their peace; not to eat of all those dishes at table, which even their present health otherwise admits; nor to store their house with all those furnitures, which even their present plenty of wealth otherwise admits; nor, when they are among them that are merry, to extend themselves to all that mirth, which the present occasion of wit and company otherwise admits: but to put bounds and hoops to their joys; so will they last the longer, and, when they depart, return the sooner. If we would judge ourselves, we should not be judged; and if we would bound ourselves, we should not be bounded. But if they shall fear that, at such or such a time, their peace and mirth have carried them further than this moderation; then to take Job's admirable course, who sacrificed, lest his children should have transgressed in their mirth. So let them go, and find some poor afflicted soul, and there be bountiful and liberal; for with such sacrifices God is well pleased.

Those that the parson finds in the military state, he fortifies, and strengthens with his utmost skill.—Now, in those that are tempted, whatsoever is unruly falls upon two heads. Either they think that there is none that can or will look after things, but all goes by chance or wit: or else, though there be a great Governor of all things, yet *to them* he is lost; as if they said, God doth forsake and persecute them, and there is none to deliver them.

If the parson suspect the first, and find sparks of such thoughts now and then to break forth, then, without opposing directly (for disputation is no cure for atheism), he scatters in his discourse three sorts of arguments; the first taken from nature, the second from the law, the third from grace.—For *nature,* he sees not how a house could be either built without a builder, or kept in repair without a house-keeper. He conceives not possibly how the winds should blow so much as they can, and the sea rage so much as it can; and all, not only without dissolution of the whole, but also of any part, by taking away so much as the usual seasons of summer and winter, earing and harvest. Let the weather be what it will, still we have bread; though sometimes more, sometimes less; wherewith also a careful Joseph might meet. He conceives not possibly how he, that would believe a divinity if he had been at the creation of all things, should less believe it, seeing the preservation of all things. For preservation is a creation; and more, it is a continued creation, and a creation every moment.—Secondly, for *the law,* there may be so evident, though unused a proof of divinity taken from thence, that the atheist or Epicurean can have nothing to contradict. The Jews yet live, and are known. They have their law and language bearing witness to them, and they to it. They are circumcised to this day; and expect the promises of the scripture. Their country also is known; the places and rivers travelled unto and frequented by others, but to them an unpenetrable rock, an unaccessible desert. Wherefore, if the Jews live, all the great wonders of old live in them; and then who can deny the stretched out arm of a mighty God? especially since it may be a just doubt, whether, considering the stubbornness of the nation, their living then in their country under so many miracles were a stranger thing, than their present exile, and disability to live in their country. And it is observable, that this very thing was intended by God; that the Jews should be his proof and witnesses, as he calls them (Isa. xliii. 12). And their very dispersion in all lands was intended, not only for a punishment to them, but as an exciting of others, by their sight, to the acknowledging of God and his power (Ps. lix. 11); and therefore this kind of punishment was chosen rather than any other.—Thirdly, for *grace*. Besides the continual succession, since the gospel, of holy men who have borne witness to the truth (there being no reason why any should distrust St. Luke, Tertullian, or Chrysostom, more than Tully, Virgil, or Livy); there are two prophecies in the gospel, which evidently argue Christ's divinity by their success. The one, concerning the woman that spent the ointment on our Saviour; for which he told, that it should never be forgotten, but with the gospel itself be preached to all ages (Matt. xxvi. 18). The other, concerning the destruction of Jerusalem; of which our Saviour said, that that generation should not pass, till all was fulfilled

(Luke xxi. 32): which Josephus' history confirmeth, and the continuance of which verdict is yet evident. To these might be added the preaching of the gospel in all nations (Matt. xxiv. 14); which we see even miraculously effected in these new discoveries, God turning men's covetousness and ambitions to the effecting of his word. Now a prophecy is a wonder sent to posterity, lest they complain of want of wonders. It is a letter sealed, and sent; which to the bearer is but paper, but to the receiver and opener is full of power. He that saw Christ open a blind man's eyes, saw not more divinity, than he that reads the woman's ointment in the gospel, or sees Jerusalem destroyed.—With some of these heads enlarged, and woven into his discourse, at several times and occasions, the parson settleth wavering minds.

But if he sees them nearer desperation than atheism—not so much doubting a God, as that he is theirs—then he dives into the boundless ocean of God's love, and the unspeakable riches of his loving kindness. He hath one argument unanswerable. If God hate them, either he doth it as they are creatures, dust and ashes; or as they are sinful. As creatures, he must needs love them; for no perfect artist ever yet hated his own work. As sinful, he must much more love them: because, notwithstanding his infinite hate of sin, his love overcame that hate ; and with an exceeding great victory, which in the creation needed not, gave them for love, even the Son of his love out of his bosom of love. So that man, which way soever he turns, hath two pledges of God's love (that in the mouth of two or three witnesses every word may be established): the one in his being, the other in his sinful being: and this, as the more faulty in him, so the more glorious in God. And all may certainly conclude that God loves them, till either they despise that love, or despair of his mercy. Not any sin else, but is within his love; but the despising of love must needs be without it. The thrusting away of his arm makes us only not embraced.

CHAPTER XXXV.
The Parson's Condescending.

THE Country Parson is a lover of old customs, if they be good and harmless: and the rather, because country people are much addicted to them; so that to favor them therein is to win their hearts, and to oppose them therein is to deject them. If there be any ill in the custom, that may be severed from the good, he pares the apple, and gives them the clean to feed on.

Particularly, he loves procession, and maintains it; because there are contained therein four manifest advantages. First, a blessing of God for the fruits of the field: secondly, justice in the preservation of bounds: thirdly, charity in loving, walking, and neighborly accompanying one another; with reconciling of differences at that time, if there be any: fourthly, mercy in relieving the poor by a liberal distribution and largess, which at that time is or ought to be used. Wherefore he exacts of all to be present at the perambulation: and those, that withdraw and sever themselves from it, he mislikes and reproves as uncharitable and unneighborly; and, if they will not reform, presents them. Nay, he is so far from condemning such assemblies, that he rather procures them to be often; as knowing that absence breeds strangeness, but presence, love. Now love is his business and aim. Wherefore he likes well that his parish at good times invite one another to their houses; and he urgeth them to it. And sometimes where he knows there hath been or is a little difference, he takes one of the parties, and goes with him to the other; and all dine or sup together. There is much preaching in this friendliness.

Another old custom there is of saying, when light is brought in—" God send us the light of heaven!" and the parson likes this very well. Neither is he afraid of praising or praying to God at all times, but is rather glad of catching opportunities to do them. Light is a great blessing; and as great as food, for which we give thanks: and those that think this superstitious, neither know superstition nor themselves. As for those that are ashamed to use this form, as being old and obsolete, and not the fashion, he reforms and teaches them, that at baptism they professed not to be ashamed of Christ's cross, or for any shame to leave that which is good. He that is ashamed in small things, will extend his pusillanimity to greater. Rather should a Christian soldier take such occasions to harden himself, and to further his exercises of mortification.

CHAPTER XXXVI.

The Parson Blessing.

THE Country Parson wonders that blessing the people is in so little use with his brethren; whereas he thinks it not only a grave and reverend thing, but a beneficial also. Those who use it not, do so either out of niceness, because they like the salutations, and compliments, and forms of worldly language better;—which conformity and fashionableness is so exceeding unbefitting a minister, that it deserves reproof, not refutation;—or else, because they think it empty and superfluous. But that which the apostles used so diligently in their writings, nay, which our Saviour himself used (Mark x. 16), cannot be vain and superfluous. But this was not proper to Christ or the apostles only, no more than to be a spiritual father was appropriated to them. And if temporal fathers bless their children, how much more may, and ought, spiritual fathers! Besides, the priests of the Old Testament were commanded to bless the people; and the form thereof is prescribed (Num. vi.). Now, as the apostle argues in another case, if the ministration of condemnation did bless, how shall not the ministration of the Spirit exceed in blessing? The fruit of this blessing good Hannah found, and received with great joy (1 Sam. i. 18), though it came from a man disallowed by God: for it was not the person, but priesthood, that blessed; so that even ill priests may bless.—Neither have the ministers power of blessing only, but also of cursing. So, in the Old Testament, Elisha cursed the children (2 Kings ii. 24); which though our Saviour reproved, as unbefitting for his particular, who was to shew all humility before his passion, yet he allows it in his apostles. And therefore St. Peter used that fearful imprecation to Simon Magus (Acts viii.),—*Thy money perish with thee:* and the event confirmed it. So did St. Paul (2 Tim. iv. 14, and 1 Tim. i. 20); speaking of Alexander the coppersmith, who had withstood his preaching, *The Lord,* saith he, *reward him according to his works.* And again, of Hymeneus and Alexander he saith, he had *delivered them to Satan, that they might learn not to blaspheme.* The forms both of blessing and cursing are expounded in the common prayerbook; the one, in "The grace of our Lord Jesus Christ," &c. and "The peace of God," &c.: the other in general in the Commination.

Now blessing differs from prayer, in assurance; because it is not performed by way of request, but of confidence and power, effectually applying God's favor to the blessed, by the interesting of that dignity wherewith God hath invested the priest, and engaging of God's own power and institution for a blessing. The neglect of this duty in ministers themselves, hath made the people also neglect it; so that they are so far from craving this benefit from their ghostly father, that they oftentimes go out of church before he hath blessed them.—In the time of popery, the priest's *benedicite* and his holy water were over-highly valued; and now we are fallen to the clean contrary; even from superstition to coldness and atheism.—But the parson first values the gift in himself, and then teacheth his parish to value it. And it is observable, that, if a minister talk with a great man in the ordinary course of complimenting language, he shall be esteemed as ordinary complimenters. But if he often interpose a blessing, when the other gives him just opportunity by speaking any good, this unusual form begets a reverence, and makes him esteemed according to his profession. The same is to be observed in writing letters also.

To conclude; if all men are to bless upon occasion, as appears (Rom. xii. 14), how much more those who are spiritual fathers.

CHAPTER XXXVII.
Concerning Detraction.

THE Country Parson,—perceiving that most, when they are at leisure, make others' faults their entertainment and discourse; and that even some good men think, so they speak truth, they may disclose another's fault,—finds it somewhat difficult how to proceed in this point. For if he absolutely shut up men's mouths, and forbid all disclosing of faults, many an evil may not only be, but also spread in his parish, without any remedy (which cannot be applied without notice), to the dishonor of God, and the infection of his flock, and the discomfort, discredit, and hindrance of the pastor. On the other side, if it be unlawful to open faults, no benefit or advantage can make it lawful; for we must not do evil, that good may come o it.

Now the parson, taking this point to task (which is so exceeding useful, and hath taken so deep root that it seems the very life and substance of conversation), hath proceeded thus far in the discussing of it. Faults are either notorious, or private. Again, notorious faults are either such as are made known by common fame; and of these those that know them may talk, so they do it not with sport, but commiseration:—or else such as have passed judgment, and been corrected either by whipping, imprisoning, or the like. Of these also men may talk; and more, they may discover them to those that know them not: because infamy is a part of the sentence against malefactors, which the law intends; as is evident by those, which are branded for rogues that they may be known, or put into the stocks that they may be looked upon. But some may say, though the law allow this, the gospel doth not; which hath so much advanced charity, and ranked backbiters among the generation of the wicked (Rom. i. 30). But this is easily answered. As the executioner is not uncharitable that takes away the life of the condemned, except, besides his office, he adds a tincture of private malice, in the joy and haste of acting his part; so neither is he that defames *him*, whom the law would have defamed, except he also do it out of rancor. For, in infamy, all are executioners; and the law gives a malefactor to all to be defamed. And, as malefactors may lose and forfeit their goods or life ; so may they their good name, and the possession thereof, which, before their offence and judgment, they had in all men's breasts. For all are honest, till the contrary be proved.—Besides, it concerns the commonwealth that rogues should be known; and charity to the public hath the precedence of private charity. So that it is so far from being a fault to discover such offenders, that it is a duty rather; which may do much good, and save much harm.— Nevertheless, if the punished delinquent shall be much troubled for his sins, and turn quite another man, doubtless then also men's affections and words must turn, and forbear to speak of that, which even God himself hath forgotten.

THE END.

THE

AUTHOR'S PRAYER BEFORE SERMON.

O ALMIGHTY and ever living Lord God! Majesty, and Power, and Brightness, and Glory! How shall we dare to appear before thy face, who are contrary to thee, in all we call thee? For we are darkness, and weakness, and filthiness, and shame. Misery and sin fill our days. Yet art thou our Creator, and we thy work. Thy hands both made us, and also made us lords of all thy creatures; giving us one world in ourselves, and another to serve us. Then didst thou place us in paradise, and wert proceeding still on in thy favors, until we interrupted thy counsels, disappointed thy purposes, and sold our God—our glorious, our gracious God—for an apple. Oh, write it—oh, brand it in our foreheads for ever! For an apple once we lost our God, and still lose him for no more; for money, for meat, for diet. But thou, Lord, art patience, and pity, and sweetness, and love; therefore we sons of men are not consumed. Thou hast exalted thy mercy above all things, and hast made our salvation, not our punishment, thy glory; so that then, where sin abounded, not death, but grace superabounded. Accordingly, when we had sinned beyond any help in heaven or earth, then thou saidst, " Lo, I come !" Then did the Lord of life, unable of himself to die, contrive to do it. He took flesh, he wept, he died; for his enemies he died; even for those that derided him then, and still despise him. Blessed Saviour! many waters could not quench thy love, nor no pit overwhelm it. But, though the streams of thy blood were current through darkness, grave, and hell; yet by these thy conflicts, and seemingly hazards, didst thou arise triumphant, and therein madest us victorious.

Neither doth thy love yet stay here. For this word of thy rich peace and reconciliation thou hast committed—not to thunder or angels—but to silly and sinful men; even to me, pardoning my sins, and bidding me go feed the people of thy love.

Blessed be the God of heaven and earth, who only doth wondrous things. Awake, therefore, my lute and my viol! awake all my powers to glorify thee! We praise thee, we bless thee, we magnify thee for ever. And now, O Lord! in the power of thy victories, and in the ways of thine ordinances, and in the truth of thy love, lo! we stand here; beseeching thee to bless thy word, wherever spoken this day throughout the universal church. Oh, make it a word of power and peace, to convert those who are not yet thine, and to confirm those that are. Particularly, bless it in this thine own kingdom, which thou hast made a land of light, a storehouse of thy treasures and mercies. Oh, let not our foolish and unworthy hearts rob us of the continuance of this thy sweet love: but pardon our sins, and perfect what thou hast begun. Ride on, Lord, because of the word of truth, and meekness, and righteousness; and thy right hand shall teach thee terrible things.—Especially, bless this portion here assembled together, with thy unworthy servant speaking unto them. Lord Jesu, teach thou me, that I may teach them. Sanctify and enable all my powers, that in their full strength they may deliver thy message reverently, readily, faithfully, and fruitfully. Oh, make thy word a swift word, passing from the ear to the heart, from the heart to the life and conversation; that, as the rain returns not empty, so neither may thy word, but accomplish that for which it is given.

O Lord, hear; O Lord, forgive; O Lord, hearken, and do so for thy blessed Son's sake: in whose sweet and pleasing words we say, Our Father, &c.

A PRAYER AFTER SERMON.

BLESSED be God, and the Father of all mercy, who continueth to pour his benefits upon us. Thou hast elected us, thou hast called us, thou hast justified us, sanctified, and glorified us. Thou wast born for us, and thou livedst and diedst for us. Thou hast given us the blessings of this life, and of a better. O Lord! thy blessings hang in clusters; they come trooping upon us; they break forth like mighty waters on every side. And now, Lord, thou hast fed us with the bread of life. *So man did eat angel's food.* O Lord, bless it! O Lord, make it health and strength to us!—still striving and prospering so long within us, until our obedience reach the measure of thy love, who hast done for us as much as may be. Grant this, dear Father, for thy Son's sake, our only Saviour: to whom, with thee and the Holy Ghost,—three persons, but one most glorious, incomprehensible God,—be ascribed all honor, and glory, and praise, ever. Amen.

END OF HERBERT'S WORKS.

LaVergne, TN USA
11 November 2010
204459LV00008B/39/P